6 $\frac{50}{}$

WHOSE KIDS ARE THEY ANYWAY?

WHOSE KIDS ARE THEY ANYWAY?

Religion and Morality in America's Public Schools

RAYMOND R. ROBERTS

THE PILGRIM PRESS
CLEVELAND

T*o my children,*

Harrison and Katherine

The Pilgrim Press, 700 Prospect Avenue, Cleveland, Ohio 44115
pilgrimpress.com

© 2002 Raymond R. Roberts

All rights reserved. Published 2002

Printed in the United States of America on acid-free paper

07   06   05   04   03   02   5   4   3   2   1

Library of Congress Cataloging-in-Publication Data

Roberts, Raymond R., 1958–
    Whose kids are they anyway? : religion and morality in America's
public schools / Raymond R. Roberts.
        p.   cm.
    Includes bibliographical references (p.) and index.
    ISBN 0-8298-1457-4 (alk. paper)
    1. Moral education—United States.   2. Public schools—
United States.   I. Title.

LC311 .R53   2002
370.11'4'0973—dc21   2002019089

CONTENTS

FOREWORD

The creative young pastor-scholar Raymond Roberts offers here a careful, balanced, and accessible overview of the debates raging about how to educate our children. Critiques of public education today have led to various efforts to compensate for past injustices, reintroduce prayer and moral instruction into the curriculum, develop charter schools, provide vouchers to be used in private, parochial, and public schools, demand testing for teachers and students, and alter funding patterns through revised taxation and distribution schemes. These debates reflect divergent views of human nature and distinctive theories of what, when, where, and why students should be taught in our complex world, and of how children of various ages learn what they need to know. They also reflect divergent moral assessments of contemporary society and thus become politicized agendas of cross-cutting views of race, sex, class, and varieties of ability.

It is, of course, not new that issues of nurturing the young should attract the attention of those with considered wisdom and conviction, as well as those with a stake in the outcome. All good parents want the best for their children and all concerned citizens recognize that a wholesome environment in which to live depends largely on having quality education available to the next generation. Plato and Aristotle recognized this. So did the authors of ancient biblical texts and many sacred writings of other great traditions. Yet the moral and spiritual content and the modes of instruction have been in contention for an equally long time. Differing philosophies of life and religious convictions press these matters in diverse directions. What is, after all, "best" for the next generation, who says what is "wholesome," and how is "excellence" to be defined?

Every member of a PTO, every member of a school board, and every pastor of a church hoping for an effective ministry to the local community would benefit from reading this book. They will find a clear and sympathetic treatment of the colliding views that are prompted by the perceived crisis in public education—from left to right to the alternative prescriptions that congregate near the middle. Many are convinced that what is most at stake is the question of moral formation, but, as the title of the book asks, who is most responsible for the kind and character of moral formation needed in our increasingly pluralistic environment? Parents? Churches, synagogues, mosques, or temples? Teachers or authors of textbooks? And which moral principles, purposes, and values should be advocated by government and which left to other parts of civil society? Indeed, one of the heated issues is whether basic principles, purposes, and values can be neatly separated from information and skill in the interpretation of data.

A reader need not agree with every conclusion toward which Ray Roberts points to gain from this work. I would personally put several points somewhat differently. Yet, this study challenges me to think things through again, and shows what objections and contrary views I am likely to encounter should I seek to set my own ideas forth. More importantly, I have gained from this study a wider range of information and perspective than I had before I read it. It is a fascinating and useful contribution to religious thought, moral reflection, and public discourse.

Max L. Stackhouse
Professor of Christian Ethics
Princeton Theological Seminary

PREFACE

The interrelation of religion, morality, and America's public schools first intrigued me while serving on a family life education community advisory task force for the Amherst County, Virginia, School Board. The process of drafting a guiding statement of community values and choosing materials for the curriculum forced me to acknowledge that the conflicted terrain of moral education was not as simple as I had once supposed.

I pursued these questions in a doctoral program at Union Theological Seminary. I continue to be grateful for Dr. Douglas F. J. Ottati and Dr. Charles M. Swezey, who provided invaluable guidance as I explored these questions in my doctoral dissertation.

I also owe a debt of gratitude to Timothy Staveteig, publisher of The Pilgrim Press, for suggesting that this analysis be incorporated into a book to address educational questions raised in the 2000 presidential campaign and for his editorial advice. I owe special thanks to my wonderful agent and good friend Alice McElhinney, without whose hard work and guidance this manuscript would not have been finished. Every author should be so blessed. I am also indebted to Dr. Thomas McElhinney for his numerous suggestions as the manuscript developed, especially for his help in clarifying and structuring my argument in chapter 7. I also thank Robert Small for proofreading the manuscript and offering helpful advice. A note of thanks needs to be made to

Dr. Max Stackhouse, whose writing on the spheres and suggestions concerning public education provided critical direction to the development of my own understanding. I am also grateful to the members of Grace Presbyterian whose example, thoughtfulness, and insight have enriched and inspired me.

Finally, I am very grateful for my wife, Sallie, whose love, encouragement, patience, and proofreading made this book possible. I owe special thanks to my children, Harrison and Katherine, who allowed me to write and were a continual source of inspiration.

Acknowledgements are a way that we show our dependence on others and, through these, on the Other we call God. Through acknowledgement, we count our blessings, calculate our indebtedness, and express our gratitude. Indeed, acknowledging one's debts is never finished. Although many have made this book possible, the errors, shortsightedness, and faults of argument belong to me alone. To God be the glory.

1 | CRISIS OF CONFIDENCE

A deep crisis of confidence threatens American public education. Many question the ability of public schools to perform their basic mission to educate students. This crisis of confidence has been building for some time. A number of reports released in the mid-1980s, such as the "A Nation at Risk" report, claimed that America's public schools were failing. In nearly every statehouse across America, these reports spawned a remarkable national movement to restore excellence in public education that continues to this day. For example, in the 2000 presidential campaign, George W. Bush called for a system of national testing to hold public schools accountable.

It has been nearly twenty years since these reforms first began; yet studies reveal little progress. SAT scores remain flat. Surveys continue to show that large numbers of American teenagers do not know basic history and geography.[1] Today a growing chorus of voices calls for breaking up the "public school monopoly." They claim that public education is failing and cannot be reformed. They advocate a range of proposals from choice within public schools, to charter schools, to school vouchers, to ending public education altogether. They are being heard. Thirty-seven states

1. Sonja Barisic, "Among Teens, A Truth not so Self-evident," *The Philadelphia Inquirer*, Tuesday, 3 July 2001, A2.

have passed some sort of school choice legislation. Five other states are considering school choice proposals. Since 1998 the number of charter schools has more than doubled and is growing at an accelerating rate. As of 2001, more than 2000 charter schools were operating around the country. This number promises to grow substantially as groups organize to take advantage of these new provisions.

School choice is not the only indicator of a crisis of confidence in American public education. Entrepreneurial schools such as Chris Whittle's Edison Schools and the Knowledge Universe Learning Group, a for-profit Internet school headed by former U.S. Secretary of Education William Bennett, offer themselves as alternatives to failing public schools. In addition, the National Home Education Research Institute estimates that home schooling is growing at an annual rate of 7 to 15 percent. These trends reveal that American public education is experiencing a crisis of confidence unlike any it has experienced in its history.

Jeanne Allen, president of the Center for Education Reform, a national school choice advocacy group, sums up the crisis this way, "I don't think most parents start out wanting to start a new school; they just want the school to do what they thought the school was going to do."[2]

Americans ought to be deeply concerned about this crisis because so much is at stake. Public education is one of the most important things that Americans do together. Since the founding of the nation, people have viewed public education as an important means to a free, democratic society. Most Americans learn the story of American history and America's experiment in democracy in the classroom of a public school. Most children learn to read, write, and do computation in a public school. Public education promises to open the door of opportunity for every American to participate in economic and public life. It promises

2. "Parents Hungry for ABC's Find Schools Don't Add Up," *The New York Times*, Saturday, 28 April 2001.

to welcome diverse peoples from every social class, every ethnic heritage, and every religious persuasion and teach them the importance of working together. Finally, it promises to support an economy with a large middle class and remarkable productivity.

This book looks at all dimensions of the crisis confronting public education. It does not deny that American public education faces deep problems, but it does deny that all the problems besetting public education can be laid at the doorstep of the public school. Public schools face the same problems facing the larger society. Public education's failures are largely rooted in the failure of families, religious institutions, and the larger public to adequately support the education of children. The crisis of confidence in public education reflects the larger society's unwillingness to shoulder its educational responsibilities. Most public education critics focus too narrowly on the public school and do not pay enough attention the larger social, political, and cultural context.

To illustrate this, this book will examine the antagonistic debate over moral education in public schools. This debate is illuminating because it touches on a particularly vexing question for public schools, namely, religion. This book will show that the failure to take into account the larger picture of moral education in our society leads critics to overstate the importance of moral education in public schools. This, in turn, leads many to overestimate the significance of the public school in the moral formation of children. As a result, some make the public schools a scapegoat for the moral problems of America's youth, as they did after the shooting at Columbine High School. Others claim that because moral formation is fundamentally a religious task, school choice should be instituted to place moral formation back under religious auspices. Both responses erode confidence in public education and distract from the problems in the larger society that subvert the moral formation of young people.

This book looks at proposals for moral education in public schools to show that they are shaped by competing definitions of religion. It then shows that these definitions of religion do not adequately take into account the role of religion in society. Finally, it argues that a theory or theology of spheres provides a more adequate account of religion and its role in society than the ones that are commonly advanced in the values education debate. It claims that a theory of spheres encompasses many of the concerns raised by the debate's participants and provides a better guide to understanding the role of the public school in the moral formation of children.

To substantiate these claims this book will examine five proposals for moral education in public schools as advanced by Leland Howe, Pat Robertson, Charles Leslie Glenn, Thomas Lickona, and David Purpel. These writers offer strikingly different recommendations for moral education in public schools. Leland Howe is among those who believe that public schools can morally educate students without referring to normative moral content. Pat Robertson epitomizes those who want to reestablish Christian values in public schools. Charles Leslie Glenn represents those who seek to renew moral education by creating a system of school choice that will allow parents and teachers to reconnect moral beliefs with their religious values. Thomas Lickona exemplifies others who propose that schools teach a common morality apart from particular religious beliefs. David Purpel typifies those who encourage teachers to impart shared cultural beliefs to give moral meaning in their students' lives.

Each of these policy proposals represents a distinct type or approach to moral education. In considering the typology presented here, several things need to be kept in mind. First, this book does not claim to present an exhaustive list of types. Also, though typologies help clarify arguments and disagreements, few proposals neatly fit an ideal type. Finally, to claim that theories of religion shape these proposals is not the same thing as saying that the people promoting the proposals reason in a straight line from their theories of religion to their proposals.

Some ethicists claim that policy proposals arise from a complex pattern of moral reasoning that includes four elements: anthropological assumptions, a situational analysis, moral norms, and a loyalty.[3] These categories provide a useful way to analyze and connect moral arguments and will serve as a basis for considering the impact that theories of religion exercise on the values education debate. For this reason, these elements of moral reasoning must be considered in some depth.

FOUR ELEMENTS OF MORAL ANALYSIS

The first element of moral reasoning is called an anthropological assumption. An anthropological assumption answers the question: "Who are people?" When people argue for a policy they often call to mind certain features of human nature. These may include: assumptions about human capacities and limits, assumptions about how humans are formed, assumptions about what is given in biological nature and what is nurtured by human culture, and assumptions about what motivates people and how people can be expected to generally respond. For example, prison reformers in the early nineteenth century built the penitentiary system in the hopes that they would help criminals become "penitent" and turn over a new leaf. Although their methods may seem cruel today, they had a more optimistic view of human nature than many contemporary criminologists. Some current criminologists believe that by the time young people become involved in the criminal justice system, their basic dispositions are set. They conclude that little can be done to bring criminals back into society until they reach their late fifties or sixties.

---

3. Douglas F. Ottati, "Assessing Moral Arguments: A Study Paper," Union Theological Seminary, Richmond, VA (September 1987). See also Ralph B. Potter, *War and Moral Discourse: An Introduction to Ethics* (Richmond, VA: John Knox Press, 1969); Arthur J. Dyck, *On Human Care: An Introduction to Ethics* (Nashville: Abingdon Press, 1980); Charles Mason Swezey, "What is Theological Ethics? A Study in the Thought of James M. Gustafson," (Ph.D. diss., Vanderbilt University, 1978); and James M. Gustafson, *Protestant and Roman Catholic Ethics: Prospects for Rapprochement* (Chicago: University of Chicago Press, 1978), 140.

The second element of moral reasoning is called situational analysis. It answers the question, "What's going on?" People often argue that their proposal fits the situation. For example, people will commonly describe a problem and then proffer their policy as the solution. Or, people will say that their proposal is superior to another because it takes some fact about the circumstances into account that another proposal ignores. A situational analysis consists of a series of explicit and implicit judgments about the circumstances, including: a determination of the situation's general pattern, as well as an assessment of the elements that comprise and bear down on a situation and that can be secured to enact a policy. For example, during the breakup of the former Yugoslavia, people argued about the basic pattern of the situation. Pat Buchanan claimed that religious groups in this area had been killing each other for centuries and that it was pointless for Americans to waste their time and youth trying to bring peace to this region. Others claimed that the war was a recent development, reflecting the ambitions of Serbian President Milosevic, and that the insertion of American forces could make a difference. In assessing a situational analysis, one may verify the empirical evidence and, at least potentially, falsify the predictions. Although people marshal facts in arguing about the basic pattern of a situation, a situational analysis is a value-laden construe of the circumstances.

Moral norms are the third element of moral reasoning. Moral norms are the guidelines that answer, "Why should we do this?" For example, someone may ask, "What kind of people are we if we do not help the poor?" Or someone may invoke moral maxims such as "Thou shall not kill" or the golden rule ("Do unto others as you would have them do unto you"). Moral norms often take a form that is more developed and complex than moral maxims. In medicine, for example, physicians may refer to "standards of care." Similarly, politicians may refer to "just war theory" to support their positions.

The fourth element of moral reasoning is called a loyalty. The loyalty is the person, institution, or cause that a policy serves. A loyalty is always a noun. When medical professionals confront a difficult situation in a hospital, they may advocate a plan of action in the name of a variety of loyalties. They may claim that their plan of action helps a patient or a patient's family. Or, they may advocate a plan of action because it protects a doctor, or because it advances the cause of research and medicine, or because it advances the cause of the hospital.

Chapters 3 through 6 are devoted to exploring the roles of these elements in the proposals promoted by Howe, Robertson, Glenn, Lickona, and Purpel. Each of these chapters will show the pervasive influence of theories of religion on the other elements of moral reasoning that give rise to their recommendations.

SIX ANGLES OF ANALYSIS

Chapter 2 reviews the history of the values education debate as a way of introducing the proposals for public school moral education advanced by Howe, Robertson, Purpel, Glenn, and Lickona. It examines their proposals in some depth to illustrate their distinctiveness.

Chapter 3 shows how religion figures in the anthropological assumptions of these five authors and shapes their proposals for public school moral education. It makes the case that each of these authors appeals to a coherent theory of religion that explains the phenomenon of human religion and presents a view of what people hold in common.

Chapter 4 examines the ways in which Howe's, Robertson's, Glenn's, Lickona's and Purpel's views of the situation are shaped by their theories of religion. It explores how these participants in the values education debate view the situation of American pluralism and its impact on public education. It closes with a fuller description of public education's crisis of confidence.

Chapter 5 examines the normative conceptions of education articulated by Howe, Robertson, Glenn, Lickona, and Glenn. It shows how their theories of religion shape their understandings of what is permissible in public schools. This chapter closes by drawing on their normative conceptions of education to suggest a fuller, more adequate conception of education.

Chapter 6 examines the loyalty that lies at the heart of the proposals advocated by Howe, Robertson, Glenn, Lickona, and Glenn. It presents a vision of a public debate on public school moral education and outlines rules of that debate. It then evaluates their proposals in light of their capacity to support and sustain participants in this debate.

Chapter 7 suggests that a theology or theory of spheres provides a helpful way to understand the pluralism of American society and clarifies the task of moral education in public schools in the moral formation of children. It will show that on the basis of a theology of spheres it cannot be said that children belong to parents anymore than it can be said that they belong to the public. In fact, children belong to God and are members of a plurality of spheres. The concluding chapter will also show that each sphere is called to play a limited role as a steward in the nurture and education of children. In so doing, a religious justification for secular public education will be offered.

2 | THE VALUES EDUCATION DEBATE

A merica's public education is undergoing a crisis of confidence. This is not the first such crisis that public education has faced. Unlike others, however, this crisis threatens to be more destructive of public education. This is because many are questioning the ability of public schools to carry out their basic mission. One of the most troubling causes of the current crisis is a drawn-out and inconclusive debate over public school moral education. Other causes will be discussed in chapter 4. Americans increasingly doubt that they *can* share moral values and thus doubt that they *ought* to support public schools. Reviewing the history of the values education debate will introduce the five proposals that will be examined in this book and will show how they developed.

HISTORY OF THE VALUES EDUCATION DEBATE

Americans have always debated the purpose of public education. People who established public schools in the late eighteenth and early nineteenth centuries believed that moral education was one of its chief purposes. Following the American Revolution, early proponents of public education, such as Benjamin Rush, promoted public schooling as a means to ensure that citizens acquire the principles, opinions, and manners necessary for self-government. When Massachusetts established public schools, some orthodox Protestants protested that these schools would under-mine Christian belief. Horace Mann assured them that they would teach the common faith that was shared by all. This assur-ance did not appease everyone, but it prevailed.

Roman Catholic immigration during the nineteenth century opened a new chapter in the conversation about the moral pur-poses of education. The Protestant establishment worried that the immigrants flooding America's shores were unacquainted with the traditions of representative government. They sup-ported public schools as nurseries of democracy. Roman Catholic immigrants, objecting to the pale Protestantism of the public schools, created their own schools. Over the course of the nine-teenth and into the twentieth century many public school dis-tricts abandoned Protestant practices, such as reading from the King James Bible and "Protestant" prayers.

Throughout this period these schools continued to teach tra-ditional middle-class moral virtues as a matter of course. One need look no further than the *McGuffy Readers* to get something of the flavor of public school moral education during the first century of the American experiment. At the close of the nine-teenth century, the Protestant establishment had high regard for and confidence in public education. Many, like the leaders of the Progressive Movement, looked to public schools to solve the problems that attended immigration, urbanization, and industri-alization, such as hygiene, illiteracy, poverty, and vice.

Theological and philosophical developments in the late nineteenth century changed the nature of the conversation about moral education. Scientific advances led many to question and rethink biblical sources of knowledge. Controversies over these matters split the heretofore-united Protestant churches. They also led many, especially in academia, to question the authority of the Christian tradition.

Over the course of the twentieth century, developments in philosophy occurred that cast doubt on the idea that moral and spiritual values have any objective claim on human beings. In the early part of the century, A. J. Ayre articulated a philosophy known as logical positivism. This philosophy distinguished between facts and values, teaching that reason discovered facts through the scientific investigation of the objective world. By contrast, it asserted that moral and spiritual values were emotive constructions of the subjective self-conscious. Logical positivism claimed that facts had an objective authority and basis that values lacked.

In the latter part of the century the philosophy known as post-modernism, articulated by Michel Foucault and others, became popular. It went further than logical positivism, denying the modern claim that human reason could discover objective facts about the world. It taught that all knowledge is a human construction.

Over the course of the twentieth century, advances in technology and communication shrank the world. The new electronic media concentrated the power into fewer hands, displacing traditional authorities and sources of knowledge. In particular, the public voice of religion was displaced. Television, especially, grew into an influential and inescapable presence. During this century the media felt increasingly unbound by traditional moral norms. A great influx of non-Western immigration during the closing decades of the twentieth century exposed an increasing number of Americans to non-European ways of life. Confronted with a global village in their living rooms, many questioned the given-ness of inherited ways of doing things.

During the 1950s and 60s America went through a time of unprecedented social transformation. The civil rights movement caused many to question the goodness of established institutions. Minorities and others objected to the injustice inherent in a segregated public school system. Integration of public schools, especially in the south, led to massive resistance, the creation of private, white separatist schools, and white flight from urban schools. A series of Supreme Court rulings during the 1950s and early 1960s redefined the relationship between religion and public education and placed further limits on institutionally established religious expression in public schools. These decisions challenged the then commonplace assumption among many Christians that America was a "Christian nation." Further changes were introduced as the pill and the sexual revolution altered the sanctioned views on sexual morality. Many questioned the traditional role of women and the purpose of the family. Disillusionment over the moral purpose of the country brought on by the Vietnam War and Watergate contributed to a widely perceived cultural malaise.

These theological, philosophical, technological, demographic, social, and cultural developments created a crisis of moral confidence. This crisis led to a questioning of established social norms, a new permissiveness, and growing doubts among many Americans as to whether their neighbors shared their values.

Public schools were also caught up in this crisis. During the late 1970s a method of moral education known as values clarification became popular. Its popularity was due to its promise to provide a way to engage in moral education without advocating normative moral content. The values clarification approach spawned a number of reactions. In fact, the history of moral education in public schools over the last twenty years is largely a response to the values clarification movement, growing moral pluralism, and the fear that American society was in moral decline.

The most negative reaction to values clarification came from the Christian religious right. The Christian right perceived many of the trends in the 1970s as an attack on Christian values. It declared that America was deteriorating spiritually and morally and that public schools were encouraging this trend. It took special offense at values clarification, claiming that the denial of "moral absolutes" undercut morality. In response it sought to restore normative Christian values to the classroom. In 2001, U.S. Representative Thaddeus Kirkland represented many in the Christian right when he spoke in support of his bill to put prayer back in the public schools: "We have tried metal detectors in our schools, and violence still reigns. We have tried peer counseling, and violence still reigns. Today, we say: Let's give prayer a chance."[1]

The values clarification approach produced other reactions besides that of the Christian right. During the 1990s proposals known as Outcomes Based Education (OBE) were introduced in many states. OBE was an attempt to hold public schools accountable to measurable standards of performance. OBE advocated normative moral content, which values clarification shunned. For example, one goal of OBE was to create cooperative and tolerant students. Conservative Protestants objected that it went too far in shaping the moral sensibilities of students. They criticized OBE for undercutting the moral authority of parents and for viewing the public school as a tool to remake society. Outcomes Based Education was defeated in at least nine states.

In the early 1990s the character education movement also began but, unlike OBE, it met with significant success. It seeks to have public schools teach classical moral virtues without touching on religious questions. Programs in this movement vary widely, but some lift up a "virtue of the month" and bring in speakers to talk with students about particular moral values. This movement received a boost in 1995 when the federal government set aside money to support the development of character education programs in public schools. These programs proliferated after the shooting at Columbine High School, and today at least ten states mandate some form of character education. The No Child Left Behind Act of 2001 triples federal spending for character education programs.

The character education movement has met resistance from some quarters. Afrocentric and Indiocentric (Native American) critics complain that the virtues promoted are too closely tied to Eurocentric moral categories. They criticize these categories for supporting the human mastery of nature and the accumulation

1. *Philadelphia Inquirer,* Tuesday, 8 May 2001.

of wealth. Western-based character education, they argue, promotes values that contribute to environmental devastation, the destruction of community, and the oppression of non-Western minorities.[2]

The academic educational left counters with a different criticism. It accuses the character education movement of being a reactionary response to a perceived moral decline in the culture. It condemns character education's blindness to the larger, systemic moral problems in society, such as racial, gender, and class discrimination. The educational left argues that meaningful moral education involves socializing students in a moral vision that will equip them to address social and political problems.

The most troubling development in the moral education debate is the growing chorus of voices across the political spectrum that recommends ending common schooling altogether. School choice first became part of the national conversation in the 1980s as a footnote to Reagan administration proposals to provide tuition tax credits for private and religious schools. At that time many, including conservative Protestants, dismissed school choice proposals as a Roman Catholic scheme to get public money. Since that time school choice has gained wider acceptance. In the past ten years more than half of the states in the union have studied or implemented some plan that provides for greater choice in public education. These include school choice within public school systems, charter schools, vouchers for private schools, and the complete privatization of public education. School choice figured prominently in George W. Bush's platform during the 2000 presidential election.

In their exhaustive study, Hubert Morken and Jo Rene Formicola note the tremendous rise of the school choice movement and the proliferation of school choice experiments around

2. For a discussion of Afrocentric and Indiocentric education, see Joel Spring, *Political Agendas for Education: From the Christian Coalition to the Green Party* (Mahwah, NJ: Lawrence Erlbaum Associates, 1997).

the country. Some champion competition as a tonic for academically deficient public schools. Others claim that common schooling is immoral because it violates the consciences of minorities. Morken and Formicola note a potentially momentous shift among conservative Protestants. Twenty years ago they coalesced as a political movement with the goal of restoring traditional Christian values in public schools. Today a number of leaders of the religious right are adopting a new position that seeks public funding for their academies, even as they continue to seek to restore Christian values in public schools. Morken and Formicola believe that this shift may portend great change in the future. They characterize the school choice movement as a nascent political movement. With the right spokesperson and a unified agenda it could become a national movement that ends common schooling.[3]

The debate over moral education in public schools has reached a deeply troubling point. The problem is not that Americans are debating moral education in public schools; Americans have always debated moral education in public schools. Indeed, a vigorous, on-going conversation about the content of moral education is necessary and healthy. The trouble is that a growing number of Americans thinks that this debate suggests that common schooling ought to end. Believing that Americans cannot and should not share moral values, they argue that common schooling is immoral. This doubt is one element eroding confidence in public education and leads many to advocate abandoning public education altogether.

FIVE VOICES IN THE VALUES EDUCATION DEBATE

This short history suggests something of the diversity of voices circulating in the values education debate. This book will examine specific voices in this debate. These proposals typify distinc-

3. Hubert Morken and Jo Rene Formicola, *The Politics of School Choice* (Oxford: Rowman and Littlefield Publishers, 1999).

tive approaches to moral education in public schools. To discover what these proposals entail it will be necessary to highlight the differences between their visions of effective moral education, the means they advance for renewing moral education, and the agent that they charge with implementing their vision.[4]

Leland Howe and Values Clarification

Leland Howe typifies those who advocate an approach to moral education known as values clarification.[5] He says that the purpose of moral education is to help students construct their own systems of values. Toward this end, he encourages public school teachers to help students choose, prize, and act on their own freely chosen values.

Howe believes that teachers share the task of assisting students in constructing their own system of values. The way in which they approach this task is critical to its accomplishment. Howe emphasizes the need for teachers to honor the most basic tenet of values clarification, namely, that students arrive at their own values freely, apart from any coercion. Students can only do this, he believes, when teachers adopt a stance of moral agnosticism. Ideally, neither the teacher nor the students should see the teacher as a moral instructor. Instead, both will be coseekers in the search for the best values.

The shunning of normative moral content is the characteristic feature of values clarification advocated by Howe. From Howe's perspective, this moral neutrality creates space in which students may make sense of the conflicting values and hypocrisy that surround them. Giving students permission to internalize

4. Many ethicists believe that coherent policies possess three elements: a goal, a means to accomplish the goal, and an agent who is responsible for implementing the policy. These elements serve as points of comparison in this analysis. See, for example, Potter, *War and Moral Discourse*, 23. See also Dyck, *On Human Care*, 34.
5. Other advocates of values clarification include Louis Raths, Merrill Harmin, Sidney Simon, and Howard Kirschenbaum.

and act on their own set of values enables them to become morally mature.

Howe is aware that values clarification is criticized for being "value-free," and "relativistic." He answers these charges by noting that this approach to moral education serves some normative values. These include critical thinking, considering consequences, and choosing freely. It also serves the values of rationality, creativity, justice, freedom, and equality. In this sense, he says, values clarification rejects the "laissez faire" approach to moral education that came into vogue with "cultural relativism."

He goes on to say that values clarification is unapologetically "value-free" in the sense that teachers accept all viewpoints and do not try to impose any set of values. The goal of values clarification is teaching a valuing process. He states that teachers can only do this if they avoid heavy moralizing and indoctrination.

Pat Robertson and the Restoration of Christian Values

The values clarification approach to moral education has drawn fire from several quarters, especially from leaders of the Christian right, typified in this book by Pat Robertson. Robertson believes that the aim of moral education is to impart to students the moral and spiritual heritage of a nation and a civilization. This heritage equips students with standards and principles that enable them to discern what is good, true, and beautiful. Students who don't know these standards are morally ignorant.

He claims that this is precisely the problem with public education today. America's public schools neglect and ridicule the Judeo-Christian heritage of this nation. To remedy this situation he encourages Christians to restore the theological and moral underpinnings of public education. At the national level, he calls for abolishing the Department of Education that he claims has marginalized citizens and parents and returning public schools to local control. At the local level, he urges: "Christian people . . . to wage an ongoing and relentless battle against the educational establishment in every jurisdiction in America in support of the rights of Christian values in our schools."[6]

Toward this end, he advocates policies that many characterize as "putting God back in public schools." Robertson is no educational theorist and has not worked out the implications of his position for the whole public school curriculum in any systematic fashion. At the same time, he is confident that measures such as restoring prayer, the Ten Commandments, creationism, and Biblical values to the classroom will renew moral education. The religious basis of these moral codes makes them persuasive and morally transforming. Robertson believes that restoring these Judeo-Christian standards, symbols, and moral instruction will make schools partners with parents and religious institutions in the moral education of children.

Robertson notes that his opponents object that he is imposing his religious values on others. He denies that he intends to force his faith on others or coerce members of another faith to violate their beliefs. Rather, he aims to restore the foundations of America's institutions that are derived from and strengthened by Judeo-Christian values.

It must be noted that Robertson, like some other "restorationists" of the conservative evangelical persuasion, has begun to call for school choice. This may be a concession to his growing perception that he will not get public schools to endorse his religious and moral values. Although his more recent writings indicate a shifting of perspective, he continues to support the restoration of Judeo-Christian values as a way to renew moral education in public schools.

Mediating Types

For the purposes of this book, the "values clarification" type and the "restorationist" type are considered polar opposites. Howe

6. Pat Robertson, *The New Millennium: 10 Trends that Will Impact You and Your Family by the Year 2000* (Dallas: Word Publishing, 1990), 178.

urges teachers to teach a method of valuing and to avoid all normative content. Robertson recommends that Christians restore normative Christian content to the schools. Howe advocates individual determination of religious and moral values, whereas Robertson seeks to determine the moral and spiritual values of students.

Three proposals explicitly seek a middle way between these two poles. On the one hand, these proposals share a conviction that public school moral education has been damaged by approaches to moral education, such as values clarification, that shun normative content. They agree that values are chosen and character is formed in moral communities and they want public schools to be regarded as moral communities that exhibit and transmit normative values.

On the other hand, these three proposals explicitly seek to uphold the First Amendment's prohibition against establishing a particular religion. Their proponents claim that they accomplish this in a way that a restorationist does not. Although they vary considerably on what counts as indoctrination, none believes that any particular religion, not even his own, should be imposed on others through the public schools. They encourage public schools to respect the religious plurality of American society.

Charles Glenn and School Choice

Charles L. Glenn typifies those who believe that the only way to renew moral education is to create a system of school choice.[7]

7. Other proponents with a similar viewpoint include: Rockne McCarthy, James W. Skillen, and William Harper, *Disestablishment a Second Time: Genuine Pluralism for American Schools* (Grand Rapids: Christian University Press, 1982); Richard John Neuhaus, ed., *Democracy and the Renewal of Public Education* (Grand Rapids: Eerdmans Publishing, 1987); James W. Skillen, *Recharging the American Experiment: Principled Pluralism for Genuine Civic Community* (Grand Rapids: Baker Books, 1994); and Stanley Hauerwas and John H. Westerhoff, eds., *Schooling Christians: "Holy Experiments" in American Education* (Grand Rapids: Eerdmans Publishing, 1992). See also Myron Lieberman, *Public Education: An Autopsy* (Cambridge, MA: Harvard University Press, 1993).

Glenn's proposal affirms something of both Howe and Robertson. He shares with Howe a belief that it is wrong for public school teachers to impose normative moral and religious values on students. With Robertson, he shares a belief that education requires transmitting normative moral and religious content.

Glenn thinks that this creates a dilemma for public schools. They cannot do both. Glenn solves this dilemma by advocating a system of government-run school choice. According to Glenn, a system of school choice promises to renew moral education by enabling parents and teachers to come together around a shared religious vision of life and work together to form the character of students. Schools chosen by parents and teachers will possess a distinctive ethos shaped by their shared moral and religious beliefs. Such an ethos, he says, is an important condition and requirement for moral formation.

Glenn knows that many people object that school choice will dismantle public education. When these people warn of white supremacist and Nazi schools, he accuses them of engaging in scare tactics. Most democratic countries, he counters, allow religious choices in schooling. Experiments in school choice that he has been associated with in Boston demonstrate that a program of school choice can work in the United States. He is confident that Americans can construct a system of school choice that will renew important public goods such as universal literacy and racial integration.

Note, Glenn is not advocating a "hands-off" approach to school choice. Instead he maintains that government-run school choice needs to embody and express the will of the public. Schools that receive public funding need to serve the common goals of society. In fact he condemns those advocates of school choice who call for a "free market" in education. An improperly conceived system of school choice, Glenn cautions, will subvert the common values and goals education should serve.

The crucial question here is precisely what these goals should be. On this question he is not entirely clear. On the one hand he supports a national curriculum that would create a uniform system for measuring instructional outcomes. He also thinks that schools should further the social goals of racial, ethnic, linguistic, and class integration.

On the other hand, he admits that he is uncertain whether civic virtue should be included among these goals. His ambivalence about civic virtue grows out of his belief that society lacks a consensus about civic virtue. He thinks that the public generally agrees on the skills and subject matter they want all students to learn. He thinks that this consensus provides a basis for instituting a national curriculum and national testing. Glenn does not believe, however, that civic virtue enjoys this same consensus. He says that if schools are to be held accountable for civic virtue, the state should not dictate the teaching process or "the context of meaning, the 'symbolic universe,' within which students are taught."[8]

Glenn identifies the state as the agent responsible for creating and administering a system of school choice. In his book, *The Ambiguous Embrace: Government and Faith-Based Schools and Social Agencies,* he spells out detailed guidelines for structuring a relationship between the state and religious schools.[9] A good system of school choice, according to Glenn, will have several features. It will possess a system of parental outreach and counseling that informs and empowers parents concerning their educational options. It will also have a strategy to make certain that every school is effective, so that no "bad" choices are available.

At the same time, he cautions that these regulations and requirements should not become so burdensome that they quash legitimate diversity, including religious diversity. For school choice to work, he says, schools must be free to pursue their own

---

8. Charles Leslie Glenn, *The Myth of the Common School* (Amherst: University of Massachusetts Press, 1986), xi.
9. Charles Leslie Glenn, *The Ambiguous Embrace: Government and Faith-Based Schools and Social Agencies* (Princeton, NJ: Princeton University Press, 2000).

vision of education. They can only do this if the state's authority and oversight is limited. Government should not be allowed to strangle private education with bureaucracy. He also says that the state must honor a school's right to define its own mission and to choose the means to accomplish it. Private schools, Glenn says, need permission to discriminate in hiring on the basis of religious belief. Otherwise religious schools will not have teachers and staff who support their religious vision and purpose.

Thomas Lickona and Educating for Character

Thomas Lickona also strikes a unique middle way between the poles of educating without normative values and restoring normative Christian spiritual and moral values. His proposal typifies those approaches that advocate teaching the common morality apart from religion.[10] Like Robertson and Glenn, Lickona distinguishes his proposal from approaches to moral education, such as values clarification, that do not commit the school to saying some things are right and other things are wrong. Unlike Glenn and Robertson, however, he believes that public schools can engage in meaningful moral education without appealing to a religious worldview.

Lickona urges public schools to educate for character by teaching the moral values that everyone shares, regardless of their religious persuasion. His proposal has two parts. First, he encourages public schools to develop a consensus among parents and in the larger community around the common moral values of respect and responsibility. He encourages schools to build a con-

---

10. Other figures in the character movement include William Kilpatrick, *Why Johnny Can't Tell Right from Wrong: And What We Can Do About It* (New York: Simon and Schuster, 1992); Robert D. Heslep, *Moral Education for America* (Westport, CT: Praeger Publishers, 1995); Dr. Philip Fitch Vincent, *Rules and Procedures for Character Education: The First Step toward School Civility* (Chapel Hill, NC: Character Development Publishing, 1999);and Rita Stein, Roberta Richin, Richard Banyon, Francine Banyon, and Marc Stein, *Connecting Character to Conduct: Helping Students Do the Right Things* (Alexandria, VA: Association for Supervision and Curriculum Development, 2000).

sensus by bringing parents together to discuss common values and suggests ways that public schools can facilitate conversations that will rebuild a value consensus around the school. He notes that these conversations have enlisted parents as supporters of and partners in the moral education of their children. This, in turn, has increased the effectiveness of the schools' program of moral education.

Once schools secure this consensus, he says that schools should explicitly teach a curriculum of moral education. In this curriculum respect and responsibility are the "fourth and fifth Rs." Although respect and responsibility form the core of the moral curriculum, he believes that schools must also teach other attendant moral values. These include: fairness, tolerance, prudence, courtesy, honesty, helpfulness, compassion, cooperation, courage, kindness, and self-control. Virtues such as these help students flesh out what it means to act respectfully and responsibly and give content to character education. He urges schools to teach these values so as to shape every aspect of the student: so that they know the good, desire the good, and do the good. He urges schools to convey to students that these moral values are not subjective preferences, but that they have an objective claim on the individual and collective conscience. Students should appreciate that not living by these values constitutes real moral failure.

Although teachers figure prominently in his proposal and many of his recommendations counsel teachers on the ways in which they can engage in moral education, Lickona identifies public schools as the agent that should implement his policy. Moral education is the responsibility of the whole school because every aspect of the curriculum and the operation of the school can and should serve the purpose of forming character. Schools must recreate a value consensus that supports the moral education of students. This is beyond the ability of individual teachers. Schools should coach every teacher so that he or she sees himself or herself as a "caregiver, model, and mentor" and so that every teacher is able to utilize the whole curriculum for moral education. Schools should seek to utilize every aspect of classroom and school life for character education. In his book, *Educating for Character,* he catalogues an exhaustive list of methods, strategies, and advice.[11] These include ideas for creating democratic classrooms and recommendations for addressing controversial issues such as abortion and homosexuality.

Lickona responds to those who accuse him of advocating moral indoctrination by saying that "indoctrination" is a scare word. It implies that public schools will push a sectarian view. It suggests that educators will not permit critical thinking or respect the human rights of students. He counters this charge by recalling an earlier meaning of indoctrination that defined it as "instruction in rudimentary principles." Public schools, he says, ought to engage in this earlier meaning of indoctrination by directly instructing students in right conduct.

David Purpel and Teaching for Meaning

David Purpel's recommendation is the most complex and far-reaching of the proposals being examined. Typical of many proposals coming from the academic left, his proposal touches on the purpose of education in light of broad cultural and great societal questions.[12] He accuses Thomas Lickona, and other members of the character education movement, of advocating immoral education. Purpel blasts them for never questioning the ways in which privilege, competition, and domination drive education. He lambastes them for their narrow preoccupation with the personal morality of individuals and for never pondering the immorality of the social and political structures of society. He accuses them of

11. Thomas Lickona, *Educating for Character: How Our Schools Can Teach Respect and Responsibility* (New York: Bantam Books, 1991).
12. Other writers with similar views include Jerome Bruner, *The Culture of Education* (Cambridge, MA: Harvard University Press, 1996); Robert T. Sandin, *The Rehabilitation of Virtue: Foundations of Moral Education* (New York: Praeger Publishers, 1992); and David Trend, *The Crisis of Meaning in Culture and Education* (Minneapolis: University of Minnesota Press, 1995).

encouraging social passivity and immoral complacency. Purpel says that a truly moral program of education would be far different. It would foster outrage at the ways that culture values success, materialism, and individual achievement at the expense of community. It would understand that its first purpose is to solve the problems of hunger, inequality, violence, and environmental degradation. In short, it would seek to create a better world.

Purpel proposes that teachers renew moral education and create a better world by "teaching for meaning." Teaching for meaning goes well beyond Lickona's recommendation that schools teach the common morality. Purpel wants teachers to give students a moral vision that will transform the common morality. Teachers can do this by introducing their students to culture's highest religious beliefs.

Purpel's proposal involves two moves. The first entails renewing the common cultural religion and contributing to the creation of a "grand consensual myth." The second comprises acquainting students with the culture's common religious substance. Regarding the first move, he tells educators that they cannot and must not simply be neutral in regards to the great human questions: What is the purpose of life? What is sacred? How should one respond to the crises that threatens human existence? He declares that they must accept that education transmits culture and that they bear responsibility for the state of culture. This means that they must understand that their foremost responsibility is generating a persuasive belief system that promises to build a joyful community for all. Purpel tells teachers that they can only do this if they utilize the language of vision and meaning, which is the language of religion. He recognizes that some teachers may be reluctant to do this, but he urges them to be bold.

> [Educators] must not allow this [religious] impulse or the language of this impulse to become the sole property of a separate and distinct group of clergy, theology professors, or churchgoers. We must recover the language of

religion and metaphysics as integral parts of our individual and communal searches for meaning, even though this can and will continue to create discomfort for those of us educated to be skeptical if not scornful of religious inquiry.[13]

Teachers, he argues, should take up the urgent task of transforming basic cultural institutions and belief systems. They should lead the way in creating a vital, authentic, and energizing vision of meaning. Teachers should not think of themselves as dog-soldiers that merely execute the wishes of their superiors, but view themselves as cultural leaders. Teachers can exercise cultural leadership by committing themselves to a vision of what is sacred and ultimate. In so doing they can become prophets who critique the culture and the educational system the culture has produced. Purpel lifts up three "significant forums" where teachers can exercise cultural leadership: the classroom, their relationships with students' parents, and their interaction with other teachers and professionals.

Purpel's second move involves his understanding of cultural leadership in the classroom. Cultural leadership in the classroom entails helping students become acquainted with culture's common religious substance. By introducing students to America's highest cultural beliefs, educators give students moral vision and purpose. Students with moral vision will be equipped to address the great social, economic, and environmental challenges that Purpel believes jeopardize the human future.

Teachers can and should engage in moral education, but Purpel insists that moral education is not enough. Unlike the character educators, Purpel does not want to form students who will get along well in society. He wants to empower students to change society. Students can only change society if they have a

---

13. David Purpel and James B. MacDonald, "Curriculum and Planning: Visions and Metaphors," *Journal of Curriculum and Supervision* 2, no. 2 (winter 1987): 186.

moral vision that transcends and critiques corrupt cultural norms, patterns, and institutions.

This means that not just any moral vision will do. He says that "critical rationality and self-awareness" cannot create a more just and caring world. The same goes for all the tired, empty pieties about preserving civilization, capitalism, liberalism, or the enlightenment. These concepts have served their time and are unable to provide new direction or sustain any beneficial energy. He urges teachers to draw on their culture's myths, narratives, and traditions to generate a new vision of caring and outrage. If teachers will seize the moment, they have:

> a marvelous opportunity to participate in [the] most important cultural project of our time—the creation of a renewed common vision. . . . Elements of this vision are available from our traditions of fundamental commitments to love, human dignity, and social justice grounded in a quest for a life of meaning. An education that is fully dedicated to this quest is what will make it moral. Nothing else will do.[14]

Purpel articulates an "emerging myth" that he suggests can serve as a new common moral vision. This myth is an amalgamation of four diverse cultural traditions, two ancient and two modern. He says teachers may appropriate from the Socratic tradition a belief in the sacredness of critical thinking. And, from the Prophetic tradition in the Bible, they may find an enduring commitment to justice and a vision of an alternative society. In addition, Liberation Theology, which is a recent theological development that originated in the Third World, is a reminder that caring for the needy is more important than the accumulation of wealth and the exercise of power. Its virtue, he tells us, is that it takes Jesus' teachings seriously, "apart from any theological inter-

---

14. David Purpel, "Moral Education: An Idea Whose Time Has Gone," *The Clearing House* 64 (May/June 1991): 311.

pretation." Finally, Creation Theology, as articulated by Matthew Fox, contributes a sense that the environment is sacred and supports collective and responsible action on its behalf. Purpel says that these traditions support an ethic of wholeness, relationship, harmony, joy, justice, and love.

Purpel anticipates that his proposal raises serious concerns about indoctrination. He replies that concerns about indoctrination simply remind everyone of the nature of crisis, which is the difficulty of creating a vital and energizing vision of meaning in the midst of significant pluralism, skepticism, and nihilism.

He offers no apologies for being explicit about the place of values and beliefs in education. Teachers have no choice but to address beliefs and values. In education beliefs and values are unavoidable. Furthermore, teachers must address questions of meaning because the danger of dogmatism and indoctrination pale in comparison with the perils of remaining uncommitted. Although religion is "a risky and dangerous zone filled with land mines," it is also "populated by time bombs." Avoiding religion is thus more dangerous than dealing with it. If educators fail to address the difficult problem of religion, civilization, and possibly humanity itself, will die.

Purpel truly believes that teachers can help reconstruct an over-arching religious mythos without offending religious sensibilities, in part because the fear of dogmatism, indoctrination, manipulation, and the imposition of teacher values upon students are, themselves, cultural values. He reminds teachers that they are educators, not indoctrinators. Teachers are moral leaders, not politicians. They lead by persuasion, not force. They do not propagate dogma. They can and should lead their students in an examination of important religious and moral issues.

EFFECTIVE MORAL EDUCATION?

Each of these writers recommends a different means to make the public schools effective at moral education. Howe advises teachers to avoid normative values and to teach their students a valuing process. Robertson urges Christians to restore the traditional theological and moral content of public education. Glenn encourages the public to create a system of school choice. Lickona recommends that schools educate for character by teaching shared moral values and leaving religion out of it. Purpel proposes that teachers give their students a moral vision by introducing them to the religious dimensions of culture.

These proposals for moral education represent the major alternatives in the values education debate. This book contends that each of these proposals reflects a distinctive understanding of religion and human nature. In order to understand the pervasive influence of their views of religion, the anthropological assumptions articulated by Howe, Robertson, Glenn, Lickona, and Purpel need to be analyzed.

3 | RELIGION AND HUMAN NATURE

Some people call for reestablishing prayer in schools as a means of moral education. Others insist that prayer is not permissible in public schools. Still others urge schools to teach morality and leave religion out of it. Critics of this last approach often accuse its proponents of trying to sneak a religion of secularism in the back door. People who address public school moral education make assumptions about what Americans should and do share in the realm of moral meaning.

Anthropological assumptions are an element of moral reasoning. Policies concerning moral education in public schools may involve a number of assumptions about human nature. For example, they may include beliefs about how human beings are formed. They may include assumptions about human capacities and limits, as well as assumptions about nature and nurture, that touch on what is permissible and possible in a public school setting. Given First Amendment concerns, people who address moral education in public schools must also make suppositions about how religion figures in human life.

The proposals put forward by Howe, Robertson, Glenn, Lickona, and Purpel contain such anthropological assumptions. In what ways do these constitute a theory of religion (beliefs about religion that explains the place and role of religion in human life)? A theory of religion may narrowly identify religion with rituals and institutions. Or, it may identify religion more broadly with a dimension of human existence such as the human need for meaning. A theory of religion is useless unless it can explain significant features of all the religions. Thus, a theory of religion sets forth suppositions about how religion operates in human life, how it is transmitted from one generation to the next, and what the religions hold in common. These assumptions speak to what is universal in human nature and shared by all. They also speak to what is particular to individuals and groups. To discover the theories of religion that Howe, Robertson, Glenn, Lickona, and Purpel advance in making their proposals, it will be necessary to pay close attention to their understanding of religion's relationship to morality and to what their anthropological assumptions say that people can and should share in the realm of meaning and morality.

None of the writers examined here is a philosopher or anthropologist of religion. They are professors of education, administrators, and clergy persons who are addressing the issue of moral education in public schools. Some draw on the work of religious theorists, but none presents a well-developed, detailed, or original philosophy of religion. Even so, each of them consistently appeals to a unique and coherent view of religion.

ANTHROPOLOGICAL ASSUMPTIONS AND RELIGION

Leland Howe and the Construction of Meaning

Leland Howe emphasizes the ability of humans to construct systems of value as they mature. As people mature they decide who they are, determine their guiding moral principles, and choose what is important to them. Together, these choices constitute their values. Values, Howe indicates, provide direction for one's life. They are "the things we are for and the things we are against." If values are clear and soundly chosen, they promise to help individuals live purposeful and meaningful lives. Conversely, if values are confused, individuals will lack direction and lead frustrated lives.

Howe employs the word "values" to cover a wide-range of principles, character traits, loyalties, centers of value, and beliefs about the world. "Values" is an umbrella term that covers both religious and moral ideals. He does not draw a sharp line between them. Values are the moral principles that guide one in making moral choices, and they are the beliefs that give one's life meaning. Thus, for Howe the relationship between religion and morality remains unclear.

Central to Howe's recommendation is his belief that the purpose of education is to develop character. It is important to note that Howe's definition of character is *procedural* (how a choice is made) rather than *substantive* (the content of that choice). Moral character, for Howe, involves "making good choices." He has virtually nothing to say about the substance of the choices one makes. The flaws of character, for him, are procedural flaws. That is, they have to do with defects in the valuing process. He does not believe that people violate an objective moral standard because he does not think that an objective moral standard exists. Instead he attributes the bad things that people do to flaws in their valuing process. People suffer value confusion when they are unaware or uncertain about their values, or when they experience conflict between their values, or when they are unreflective and inconsistent in living out their most cherished values. People who are unclear about their values—whatever their values are—make bad choices.

For Howe's theory of religion, the ability to construct value systems is the universal ingredient. Although the ability and need to become good at making choices is universal, the particular systems of religious and moral values that people construct and choose have no universal significance. They are as particular and unique as the individuals who construct them. Howe does not believe any universal values are available, except perhaps the value of respect for other people's valuing process.

Pat Robertson and True Religion

Pat Robertson believes that human beings cannot be understood apart from the True and Living God. God has given people a God-shaped vacuum that leads them to search for divine communion. People are meant for divine communion. They long for divine communion, but sin prevents them from finding it. Sin leads people to rebel against God. It leads to the corruption of religion, when sinful people create false gods who will endorse and embody their base desires. Robertson's belief in human sinfulness causes him to be deeply pessimistic about the ability of human beings to grasp what is universally true. As a result, his theory of religion is not nearly as optimistic as Howe's.

Fortunately, God offers humans divine revelation in the Bible. God's revelation discloses the universal truth of things. Apart from this divine self-disclosure people are lost. They cannot identify the hunger in their lives as hunger for God. They do not know that they are accountable to a holy God who will judge them for their sins. From Robertson's perspective, Christianity is the universally true religion. Its truth does not depend on people to acknowledge it as true (or good or helpful). Apart from this truth, people tend to spiritual and moral error.

Robertson places other religions into three general categories. He considers Judaism, Islam, and Mormonism to be incomplete or corrupt versions of the true religion. They are close to the truth, but contain errors. He urges Christians to make common cause with members of these faiths, but warns that their beliefs are mistaken on important matters.

Although Robertson sometimes talks about communism, humanism, and atheism as the denial of religion, he usually refers to them as false religions. These three schools of thought share the prideful assumption that humans are the measure of all things. Because they deny God's existence they woefully diminish their estimation of human significance. They start off putting humans in the place of God, but they invariably end up equating humans with animals and denying the value of human life. The denial of human worth leads political leaders to think that troublesome people are expendable. In this way, humanism leads to human suffering and anguish. He says that the fall of communism demonstrates that the trust that millions of people put into humanist systems is misplaced. He finds little in common with adherents of these faiths. In fact, he fears them. He claims that humanists take offense at the notion that they are accountable to any authority beyond themselves. This leads them to persecute Christians, Jews, and anyone else who confesses a higher authority.

Still other religions, such as the ancient Baals, the Greek mystery religions, paganism, and Hinduism, he regards as demonic manifestations.[1] He fears that the decline of Christianity in the West has created a spiritual vacuum that has opened people to their evil influences. These religions are anathema to him.

Robertson uses "morality" to refer to moral behavior and character. Morality, for him, is doing what God wants. God reveals God's desires for human life in the Bible. God's desire for human life is discovered in moral codes such as the Ten Commandments and the Sermon on the Mount. He rejects other sources of moral authority. He is especially critical of those, like Howe, who believe that humans can construct their own systems of meaning and morality. He says that people who place moral authority in human hands exchange the verities of God for human vanity. According to Robertson, apart from God's law, people are laws unto themselves. Lacking moral understanding, they savagely plunder and destroy and live in chaos. This is the curse that follows disobedience.

Robertson believes morality is enmeshed in religion. The two cannot be neatly separated. Immorality is a spiritual problem. It arises when people deny any source of moral authority beyond themselves, their family, their party, or their nation. Cut off from God, they do what they want and find ways to justify it. By

1. Robertson, *The New Millennium*, 7, 10, 64, 65, 75, 77, 80, 84, 86.

contrast, Robertson reminds his readers that the Bible teaches in Proverbs, "The fear of the Lord is the beginning of wisdom."

Believers recognize God as the source of moral authority. They realize that they are responsible not just to themselves, their family, their company, their country, or to humanity, but to God. They understand that God reigns and that they live in a moral universe. They see that their actions have consequences for themselves and for others. They exercise an appropriate humility and seek to be obedient to God. Spiritual health leads to moral living.

On the social level, Robertson declares that God blesses the nation that honors God. A good society shares a moral consensus. Every moral consensus is supported by religion. The ethos of a good society shapes people so that they are internally motivated to do what is good. Thus, religion does what laws and courts cannot do: it promotes a society that is both free and just.

Robertson offers a unique theory of religion. He believes that the faith and moral standards revealed in scripture are universally true. The Christian perspective is for everyone, not just for Christians. Those who believe that all truth is relative are simply wrong. Those who deny the truth of Christianity are mistaken. Other secular and religious perspectives are deviations from the universally true religion and are evidence of sin. According to Robertson, this universally true perspective provides the best moral guidance and meaning to moral commitments. Apart from this perspective, human nature cannot be understood.

Charles L. Glenn and Religious Narrative

Charles L. Glenn thinks that everyone is religious. He believes that people cannot function without a narrative to make sense of their lives. Drawing on the work of Alistair McIntyre and Stanley Hauerwas, Glenn defines religion as a set of beliefs and stories that provides a "framework of meaning," a "map of reality" and a "context of meanings." Such a narrative provides "a symbolic universe" and "a coherent interpretation of reality" that helps an individual or community understand the world. Even a narrative that denies the truth of all religion, if it gives meaning to the life of the person who tells the story, constitutes, by definition, a religion.

When Glenn talks about morality, he means values, decision-making, and character. Character is a central concept for him, because he believes that education forms character. In contrast to Howe, Glenn believes that character involves substantive moral and religious content. Communities form character in light of the narrative they tell.

Glenn's view of human nature presents a unique view of what is universal and what is particular to human beings. Although he thinks the need for meaning is universal, he believes that the narratives that individuals and groups live by are always particular and incommensurable. People may point to similarities between particular religious narratives, but they can only understand the world, including other religions, from the perspective of their own guiding narrative.

This means that no nonreligious or religiously neutral perspective exists. All perspectives have religious valence. Getting beneath the veneer of religious interpretation to a more religiously neutral, universal, or more real way of looking at the world is impossible. This leads him to deny that any narrative can claim greater universality than any other. Robertson, Glenn says, may believe that his narrative is universal because it explains all things. But from the perspective of an adherent of another narrative, Robertson's perspective is merely his particular way of looking at things. Since every narrative is as particular as the community that tells it, Glenn insists that no narrative can claim greater universality than any other.

Glenn's conviction that people reason within narratives, not apart from them, explains why he denies the existence of universal reason. He rejects universal reason because the idea of rationality itself is an invention of the enlightenment narrative. Enlightenment secularism, he says, tells the story of transcending religious particularity, achieving scientific objectivity, and arriving at universal moral truth. He denies that any narrative can achieve this. Secularism, like every religion, offers a coherent interpretation of reality. Furthermore, like every religion, it rests on unproven assumptions about the nature and structure of reality. These assumptions are no more reasonable than any other religious belief. He observes that modern ethical theorists denigrate other religious narratives by insisting that all rational people are logically devoted to certain moral principles or procedures such as the "categorical imperative," the "ideal observer," "universalizability," and the "original position." They imply that people whose moral reasoning is shaped by their religious beliefs are unreasonable and cannot be trusted to act morally.[2] This explains why people who seemingly have no religious beliefs can be as intolerant as anyone else.

Glenn's belief that people depend on narratives for meaning explains why he denies the existence of universal morality. He does not think that morality can be easily separated from religion. Glenn acknowledges that people share moral values, but cautions against making too much of this commonality. Moral principles may appear, on the surface, to be identical, but this does not prove that a universal morality exists or that the narratives that give rise to them are identical. People agree, for example, that stealing is wrong, but give different reasons for why it is wrong. Such differences may seem trivial as teachers seek to explain them to elementary school children, but they grow more significant as students get older. Engaging high school students in a meaningful discussion about citizenship is difficult unless one can refer to religion. The reason? Moral values have no significance without a larger religious framework of meaning. Indeed, character has no meaning without a story or narrative to give it meaning. Glenn draws a close connection between morality and religion in his oft-used phrase, "beliefs and values."

2. Charles Leslie Glenn and Joshua Glenn, "Making Room for Religious Conviction in Democracy's Schools," in *Schooling Christians: "Holy Experiments"*, 103.

Glenn's narrative theory of religion, like Howe's, denies that religious and moral values are objective and universal. Whereas Howe considers every individual's narrative particular and unique, Glenn thinks that every community's narrative is particular and unique. This makes Glenn much more attentive to the social dimensions of religious formation than Howe. Whereas Howe emphasizes individual ability to construct a narrative, Glenn says that communities form people in a narrative. Communities pass on their narratives by telling them to children and socializing their children into the community's characteristic practices.

Thomas Lickona and Natural Law

Thomas Lickona believes that humans can know objective moral truth. He believes that all human beings have the capacity to reason and that they can use their reason to discover the natural moral law. This is the basis for the distinction he draws between religion and morality, which is greater than that of any of the other writers examined here.

When Lickona talks about morality he means values and character. Lickona distinguishes among several categories of values. The first distinction he draws is between moral and nonmoral values. Nonmoral values include things such as partiality for country over classical music, or Thai over German cuisine. Nonmoral values do not bind anyone, but are mere personal preferences. Moral values, by contrast, are morally binding.

The second distinction he draws is between universal and nonuniversal moral values. Universal moral values include treating everyone justly and respecting their rights and dignity. Universal moral values bind everyone and reflect the obligations of the universal moral law. They correlate with the universal moral law that one discovers through the use of reason.

Nonuniversal moral values are the values discovered through the use of feelings. They include religious duties such as Sabbath observance and tithing. They carry no universal obligation.

Lickona says, "I as an individual may feel a serious personal obligation [toward my religious duties] but I may not impose these personally felt obligations on others."[3]

Lickona discusses values extensively, but places greater emphasis on character. He defines character substantively, unlike Howe, telling us that it "consists of operative values, values in action." Good character involves knowing, desiring, and doing the moral law. These three dimensions of character (the intellect, the affections, and the will) interact in moral thinking, moral feeling, and moral acting.

When Thomas Lickona refers to religion, he means the historic faiths that have guided people through the centuries and that continue to guide many people today. These faiths share certain characteristics. Traditional religion, he declares, orients people in the world, identifying who they are, why they are here, and where they are going. It tells them that actions have eternal consequences and mediates divine assistance for doing the right thing. Religion also provides traditions and rituals that enable individuals and families to weave a religious vision into their private lives.

Lickona does not hide his own Catholic convictions and takes a positive approach to the great faith traditions. Lickona shares with Robertson and Glenn a belief that religion provides a vision of the purpose of human existence and, in so doing, offers the best reasons for leading moral lives. He observes that many people turn to religion for guidance, motivation, and encouragement in moral living. He cites numerous studies that correlate religious belief and moral behavior. He also notes that the moral tenets of the great religious traditions are strikingly similar. The universal natural moral law, he says, is consistent with the teachings of all great religions.

Most Americans claim some religious faith that gives meaning to life, but Lickona notes that some Americans do not claim

3. Thomas Lickona, *Educating for Character: How Schools Can Teach Respect and Responsibility* (New York: Bantam Books, 1991), 38.

to have any religious sensibilities. In striking contrast to Glenn, who thinks every person is, by definition, religious, Lickona believes that some people are nonreligious. He does not believe that religion is a universal feature of human life, and allows that some zones of life can even be relatively religion-free.

Lickona's belief in the human capacity for reason reinforces his belief that the natural law has its own logic, independent from religion. One can determine the morality of a particular action by appealing to "the classic ethical tests of reversibility (Would you want to be treated this way?) and universalizability (Would you want all persons to act this way in a similar situation?)."[4] The independent logic of morality allows one to analyze whether a particular action is moral without referring to religion at all.

Lickona's recommendation that public schools take an abstinence approach to sex education illustrates this conviction. Although some consider premarital sexual abstinence a religious value, he claims that he can demonstrate the goodness and rightness of premarital chastity through reason alone. Public schools need not mention religion at all when they teach students that this is the right approach to sexuality. Compelling nonreligious reasons for sexual abstinence abound. These include the effects of sexual intercourse on one's partner, the likelihood of a conceiving a child, and the possibility of spreading disease. He is confident that schools can define morality in rational terms that everyone will find acceptable and persuasive.

Lickona's natural law theory of religion upholds a distinctive view of what is universal and particular in human beings. Unlike Howe, he believes that universal moral values exist apart from subjective conviction. People do not construct moral values; they discover them. The fact that people are obligated to the natural

---

4. Thomas Lickona, "Is Character Education a Responsibility of the Public Schools? Yes." *Momentum* 24, no. 4 (November–December 1993): 50. See also Thomas Lickona, "The Return of Character Education," *Educational Leadership* 51, no. 3 (November 1993): 9.

law, whether or not they feel personally obliged, provides a basis for teaching morality that is lacking in Howe.

Lickona shares Robertson's belief that the universal moral law binds everyone. He differs from Robertson by denying that religion is universally binding in the same way that morality is. He places religion in the category of nonuniversal moral values. He denies that his own Catholicism has the same universal claim as the natural law.

In contrast to Glenn, Lickona does not think that moral values or moral reason is embedded in incommensurable narratives. By contrast, Lickona says that natural law is consistent with revealed religion, but has its own independent logic. He believes that people of different faiths can come together and reason morally. There are many particular religions, but there is one universal natural moral law "recognized by all civilized people and . . . taught by all enlightened creeds."

David Purpel and Civil Religion

Purpel believes that the fascinating and mysterious quality of the cosmos produces an experience of awe. This common human experience is prior to religious interpretation. Religious language develops as people seek to communicate this feeling of awe to others. Religion articulates the human experience of awe, reverence, mystical union, reorientation, and reconciliation. Religion expresses something real, namely, an individual's response to the cosmos.

Religion may mediate an experience of awe, but Purpel insists that the experience requires no particular religious stimulation or interpretation. Even atheists, he notes, claim to have experienced a sense of mystical union with the cosmos. This universal sense of the sacred quality of life accounts for humanity's enduring interest in and capacity for creating religious images and myths.

Purpel states that religion discloses the deeper patterns in life. Drawing on the thought of Ian Barbour, he claims that the myths, stories, and tenets of religion provide an imaginative construction of the universe and one's place in it. Religion explains fundamental human questions of human origin and destiny. It instructs people in the meaning of life and elevates what is truly important.

Purpel takes a striking position as compared to the other four thinkers. According to Purpel, religion is an abiding feature of culture. Drawing on sociologists of religion such as Mircea Eilade and Emile Durkheim, he claims all cultures have religious substance. The particular religious narratives in the society contribute to the universal narrative of culture and reinforce a shared sense of the sacred. This view of the sacred gives meaning to shared political, moral, and intellectual commitments. Because atheists can experience a sense of awe, it is unclear whether Purpel believes that people who consider themselves nonreligious and antireligious really are. He is convinced, however, that every culture is religious.

Purpel observes that American culture, for all its pluralism and pretensions of secularity, includes a number of concepts that involve metaphysical belief and are religious. American culture is defined by an active and lively religious tradition. A tradition of civil religiosity venerates the blessings of American heritage, democracy, and patriotic sacrifices. Public rituals such as Thanksgiving, Memorial Day, and Independence Day express this civil religion. Religion is simply a fact of cultural life.

When Purpel talks about morality he refers to both its cultural and personal dimensions. As might be expected, given the cultural slant of his thought, he pays a lot of attention to cultural morality. He worries about the immorality of American social, political, and cultural institutions. He defines cultural morality as the shared principles, rules, and ideas that govern how an individual relates to others and to the world. Purpel also thinks that morality has personal dimensions. Like every other person but Howe, Purpel defines character substantively. For him, personal character involves attitude, values, and behaviors that constitute a moral way of relating in the world. A moral person will care about social immorality.

Purpel believes that religion provides meaning and motivation for personal and cultural morality. Religion provides moral knowledge. It reveals the deep structures of the world and shows how each life is connected to others, to the environment, and to the cosmos. Especially important, for Purpel, is religion's power to criticize patterns of injustice and to help us address the challenges that threaten human existence.

Purpel's theory of religion paints a unique picture of what is universal and particular in humanity. Howe emphasizes that everyone constructs values systems. Purpel, by contrast, emphasizes that every culture constructs myths that disclose the sacred.

In contrast to Robertson, Purpel stresses the similarities between religious narratives. Purpel acknowledges differences in emphasis between religions. For example, he says that Judaism integrates morality into religion more thoroughly than Hinduism, which is more interested in metaphysical and spiritual questions. Despite these differences, he declares that "key principles and formulations . . . cut across religions, sects, denominations, and ideologies."[5] To illustrate this, he points to Mohandas Gandhi and Martin Luther King. Although Gandhi was a Hindu and Martin Luther King was a Christian, they shared a common vision of the sacred that supported them in leading movements that secured human liberation. He thinks that every particular faith possesses something of what is universally true and that no faith is without truth.

Not surprisingly, Purpel rejects Glenn's emphasis on the incommensurability of religious narratives. Purpel understands why minorities find the search for particularistic identities and cultural difference appealing, especially in light of the way that empires

5. David Purpel, *The Moral and Spiritual Crisis in Education: A Curriculum for Justice and Compassion in Education* (New York: Bergin and Garvey Press, 1989), 67.

and hegemonic majorities have crushed minority aspirations and ways of life. But he insists that stressing the radical difference between religious viewpoints is self-defeating. He warns that the principle that words have no traction in the reality of things inevitably leads to despair and nihilism. It undercuts the hard work of finding common ground and subverts the difficult task of living together. He declares that the postmodern rejection of all meta-narratives indicates the depth of crisis besetting American culture. Despite the multiple identities in this pluralistic society, he says that this culture cries out for communal vision that will support progressive social change. Glenn objects to any talk of universal narratives; Purpel urges us to talk about the "Human Narrative."

Purpel also rejects Lickona's assumptions about universal reason and the ability to discover objective moral law. Purpel warns that when reason thinks it has transcended religion, it undermines religion and confuses people about what is sacred. This robs public discourse of moral meaning. Instead, he reminds us that movements for justice and freedom have almost always been rooted in a religious vision. People need to be sustained in an alternative vision of the world that will guide and empower them to work for social change. Abstract reason is unable to do this.

THEORIES OF RELIGION

Religion figures differently in the anthropological assumptions of Howe, Robertson, Glenn, Lickona, and Purpel. Each presents a coherent approach to religion and morality that can be referred to as a theory of religion. Each theory of religion upholds a distinctive view of what is universal to all and what is particular to individuals and groups.

Howe holds a constructivist view of religion. He believes that everyone possess the capacity to construct value systems, but that the value systems that people construct are particular to the individual. No one but the person who has chosen and prized his or her religious or moral values is obligated to act on them.

Robertson believes Christianity is the universally true faith, whether people accept it or not. Humanity and morality cannot be understood apart from God's revelation. Deviation from this truth leads people into moral and spiritual error.

Glenn promotes a narrative view of religion. He believes that everyone needs a religious narrative to make sense of the world, including his or her moral commitments. Particular communities form people in narratives. Although the need for meaning is universal, no narrative can claim universality.

Lickona holds a natural law theory of religion. He believes that everyone has the capacity to reason and can use this capacity to discover the universal moral law. This moral law exists apart from our discovery. Everyone is obliged to follow the moral law. By contrast, only believers are obliged to adhere to the values of their religion.

Purpel advocates a theory of civil religion. He believes that the universal sense of the sacred gives rise to religious language. Every society possesses a culture that has religious dimensions. These religious dimensions are an amalgam of the particular religions that circulate in that society and are shared by everyone. Cultural myths give meaning to shared moral obligations.

4 | PLURALISM AND THE CRISIS OF EDUCATIONAL RESPONSIBILITY

America's growing religious, moral, and ethnic pluralism is the inescapable fact of our time, yet the meaning and significance that people attach to it varies widely. People may be thrilled about the new Ethiopian restaurant down the street. They may complain about growing immorality and the moral looseness of American culture. Or, they may complain about stifling, conforming, middle-class morality that resists coming to terms with the growing diversity of society.

This pluralism affects all of America's institutions, but it has a particularly strong impact on public education. People involved in public education must come to terms not only with the fact that people disagree on important moral and religious questions, but that they disagree about how public schools should respond to these differences. Some note the moral and religious diversity of society and insist that public schools adopt a stance of moral agnosticism. Others argue that public schools should work to eradicate immorality. Some believe that the widespread acceptance of premarital sex and the diversity of strongly felt opinion concerning its morality make the subject taboo. Others counter that these facts require public schools to take a stand.

When people argue for policies related to moral education in public schools, they often marshal social and historical data to indicate how their policy fits the general pattern of the situation. The second element of moral reasoning is situational analysis, which we defined as an interpretation of the state of affairs. A situational analysis is not a raw recitation of the "facts," but is a value-laden construe of the circumstances. For example, different viewers will select different items as most important. Such a selection has already loaded the moral assessment. Each viewer is influenced by the other elements of moral reasoning, anthropological assumptions, moral values, and loyalties. Thus, different people addressing public school moral education may draw different conclusions from the same set of facts. Specifically, they may interpret America's pluralism as values confusion or as a moral crisis or as a spiritual crisis. Their assessment of what these mean for public education may differ as well.

How, then, do Howe, Robertson, Glenn, Lickona, and Purpel view the situation in public education today? In what ways do their theories of religion influence their views of America's pluralism and its impact on public education? After these questions are answered, another broader and more adequate way of looking at the situation of public school moral education will be offered.

LELAND HOWE AND BEWILDERING PLURALISM

According to Leland Howe's theory of religion, everyone constructs a system of values as he or she matures. The ability to construct systems of meaning and morality is universal, but the systems themselves are particular and have no claim on anyone else. His theory of religion leads him to offer the most positive assessment of American pluralism and its impact on America's public schools of anyone in this study. Since he thinks that all values are particular to the individual who generates them, he does not view America's pluralism as a threat to normative values, not even his own. This leads him to be indifferent to the moral and religious pluralism of American society. In contrast to everyone else in this study, he does not think that America is suffering a moral crisis.

This is not to say that Howe believes that everything about America's pluralism is positive. He does think that it has produced values confusion among America's youth. Parents teach their children one set of values at home. They see another set of values on television. They go to church or synagogue and hear still another set of values professed. Their peers at the mall articulate yet another set of values. Widespread hypocrisy and moral inconsistency compounds this incoherence and dissonance. Parents and other authority figures say one thing and then do another.

Howe claims that this multiplicity of voices negatively impacts the moral formation of children. The moral chaos and conflict bewilders them. Confusion about the choices that confront them has led to apathy, overconforming, overdissenting, a lack of moral seriousness and commitment, and other indicators of value confusion. Since students have not constructed a coherent system of values, they have no internal guidance. Young people lack clear direction, purpose, and motivation, he tells us, because they have not chosen, prized, and acted on their own system of values.

Howe's belief that values have no universal significance leads him to be sympathetic to parents who worry that public school teachers will impose alien values on their children. This is a valid concern. In fact, he says that in a diverse and changing society, values have become a "sticky" subject for public schools. The lack of universally shared values prohibits public school teachers from imposing a single set of values on students.

More importantly, though, he says that this approach will not work. Although moral indoctrination was popular prior to World War II, America's pluralism makes it ineffective today. When teachers teach normative values, students hear them as just another voice in the chaotic mix of voices that seeks to impose values on them. Since students have not chosen them for their own, they consider the teacher's values and the school's values alien.

Forcing alien values on students—telling students that certain values are right and others are wrong—compounds the frustration and resentment that many students feel toward the school and society. It leaves students disengaged from and alienated by the educational process. This is the source of the disruption caused by many students. Moral indoctrination denies their humanity. Sensing that they are not respected, they rebel. The good news, according to Howe, is that schools don't have to impose values on students to engage in effective moral education.

PAT ROBERTSON AND THE DECLINE OF AMERICA

Pat Robertson believes that Christianity is universally true, regardless of what anyone else thinks. Apart from this truth people stray into false religion and immorality. His theory of religion leads him to offer the most pessimistic reading of the situation of anyone in this study. He finds many aspects of America's pluralism deeply troubling because he views it as a falling away from the truth. The fact that "our cities are on fire" with divorce, violence, and immorality indicates a huge spiritual crisis. People no longer know that they are accountable to God and to God's law. Robertson blames many of the troubling aspects of America's pluralism on the removal of Christian symbols and moral codes from public life, including public schools. For him, many of the Supreme Court decisions have eradicated public expressions of Christian faith and threaten true religious freedom, which is the freedom to serve the living God.

At one time, he recalls, public schools were important partners with parents and religious institutions in the moral education of children. Over the course of the twentieth century, however, this partnership unraveled. Supreme Court rulings on prayer and Bible reading "kicked almighty God out of our public schools." A cadre of well-placed "fanatical ideologues" in the education establishment removed biblical principles and values from the public schools. Robertson believes that the greatest thing anyone can do is lead a student to the universal truth of things. One can see why Robertson is disturbed that public schools no longer engage students in the universal truth.

Robertson argues that everyone can see the educational fruits of these trends. Studies repeatedly demonstrate the ineffectiveness of the public schools. Scholastic Aptitude Tests (SATs) are declining. International comparisons of educational systems regularly show America trailing other nations in mathematics, in science, and in other areas of study. In some school districts nearly half of the students do not graduate and most of those who do graduate are functionally illiterate. In contrast to Howe, who attributes student rowdiness to disengagement from the educational process, Robertson blames the current crop of rowdy, disengaged students on widespread illiteracy. He claims that for a huge number of students the course material from fourth to twelfth grades is mostly gibberish. He declares that the "educational collapse" in America's classrooms is nothing more or less than the playing out of the flawed theories of education elites.

He also claims that the trends in moral education are just as disturbing. The elimination of Christian principals and values drained education of moral content. Approaches such as values clarification, advocated by Howe, took the place of clear moral teaching. To illustrate how bad it has become, Robertson cites a teacher's manual in Alabama that says that if a student asks whether shoplifting is wrong, "You answer that you cannot tell him if shoplifting is wrong. He must decide that question for himself." He declares that such incredible nonsense shows that education is in a grip of "a group of ideological extremists who are so fixated with their illogical education theories that they have lost touch with reality."[1]

Robertson believes that moral living is grounded in the fear of God. This conviction leads him to believe that this moral crisis is rooted in a much larger spiritual crisis. Moral behavior requires self-control. Self-control implies an underlying religious

1.Pat Robertson, *The Turning Tide* (Dallas: Word Publishing, 1993), 214.

commitment. The original public schools, such as those that existed in precolonial Massachusetts, rested on this premise. Today's public schools deny this truth and America is reaping the whirlwind. The moral laxity of public education has contributed to soaring teenage birthrates, an explosive rise in sexually transmitted diseases, skyrocketing divorce rates, and a new wave of violent crime.

Robertson warns that the situation for Christians in public schools has become dire. The secular education establishment is on a "vicious vendetta." Schools don't just ignore religious values; they attack and belittle them. He tells horror stories of heavy-handed repression of Christian expression. Increasingly, humanistic or irreligious educators intrude on the relationship between Christian parents and their children. They undercut parental moral authority by teaching children alien values. They engage innocent children in foreign spiritual practices such as séances, meditation, and astral projection and expose them to evil powers and spirits. All the while, he complains, school boards see nothing wrong. Teachers and administrators are instructed to dismiss any parent who dares object as a troublemaker. He goes so far as to characterize the current trends in public education as a "war on Christianity." Fortunately, however, if Christians will respond, it doesn't have to be this way.

CHARLES LESLIE GLENN AND INSURMOUNTABLE PLURALISM

Charles Leslie Glenn believes that everyone uses a narrative to make sense of the world. Communities form persons in narratives that are as unique and incommensurable as the communities that tell them. His theory of religion leads him to think that the most significant feature of modern America is the deep and unbridgeable division created by moral and religious pluralism. He contends that as this pluralism has grown, the moral consensus that once supported common schooling has collapsed. This collapse forces Americans to decide whether all students shall be educated in common schools.

Although he believes that growing pluralism makes common schooling more difficult, he says that Americans have never been of one mind about public education. He recalls that Horace Mann, the founder of public education in Massachusetts, encountered vigorous opposition from orthodox Calvinists who considered common schooling a threat to Christian faith. Glenn claims that this opposition was staunch and unyielding. If it had not been for nativist concerns about the effects of Roman Catholic immigration upon the homogeneity and coherence of American society, disagreement over religious content would have wrecked the common school movement. He suggests that a religiously differentiated educational system would likely have developed in its place, as it did in most European nations. Instead, in the early nineteenth century as waves of Roman Catholic immigrants flooded America's shores, nervous Protestants closed ranks and rallied around the public school.

Glenn believes that Roman Catholic immigration opened a new chapter in the history of public education. Roman Catholics recognized that the pale Protestant cast of the common schools threatened their religious beliefs. In response Roman Catholics created their own schools, even while protesting religious observance in the public schools. Slowly the Protestant establishment responded to these protests by dropping overtly religious activities from the curriculum, such as reading from the King James Bible and Protestant prayers.

Significantly, Glenn does not think that eliminating these religious activities made the schools any less religious. Indeed, he thinks that during this time the mission of the school itself became more "religious." The public school became the central institution of American society, the definer of meaning, and the gatekeeper to the higher life. To question the mission of public education became "a kind of blasphemy."

According to Glenn, common schooling was possible so long as most Americans shared a general understanding of the good life and the sorts of persons they hoped their schools would form. The villages of eighteenth- and nineteenth-century New England possessed such a consensus; contemporary America does not. To back this up, he cites a study that found that public schools have no dominant set of values to uphold because communities based on residency share no set of dominant community values. Court cases and controversies over sex education in public schools provide additional evidence that Americans do not agree on moral values. But the strongest indictment of the collapse of America's moral consensus, for Glenn, is the quiet withdrawal of hundreds of thousands of children into nonpublic schools. The "acids of modernity" have dissolved the shared beliefs and values on which the common school rested and the "ravages of modernization" cannot be reversed.[2]

Glenn claims that the disintegration of a religious and moral consensus has profoundly affected moral education in schools. Schools sought to remain nonsectarian, neutral, and impartial in the face of growing pluralism. They shed distinctive religious and moral values in an effort not to offend parents. In the process, morally distinctive schools wilted into schools he describes as "wishy-washy, morally incoherent, and lowest common denominator" schools. These insipid schools are incapable of inspiring civic virtue in students.

The great irony, according to Glenn, is that religious minorities are calling the neutrality of the public school into question. These people find the purged curriculum, with all of its relativism and equivocation, inimical to their cherished beliefs and values. They challenge the notion that the common school curriculum is really neutral and nonsectarian. The litigation and controversy generated by "worldview minorities" reveals that the public school cannot achieve anything approaching a satisfactory religious "neutrality." Glenn's belief that religious narratives are unique and particular leads him to view the pluralism in society

2. Charles L. Glenn, review of "Public and Private High Schools" by James S. Coleman and Thomas Hoffer, *This World,* no. 19 (fall 1987), 126.

as resting on deep and unbridgeable differences. Although many of these disagreements seem to concern moral values, he says that if one were to press deeper, one would discover that they reflect incommensurable beliefs about the world and the place of humans in it.

Since Glenn believes all meaning is derived from religious narratives, he says that religious and moral conflict surrounding America's public schools may be viewed in two entirely contradictory ways. The controversy may be seen as the "rivalry between the claims of the particulars of family or church and the universals of the nation-state." Or, just as easily, the conflict may be seen as being between "the universals of a worldwide religious faith and the particulars of national identity."[3] According to Glenn, both are correct. It just depends on one's narrative.

Glenn's theory of religion denies that public schools can be neutral and nonsectarian. Thoroughly secular public schools send the message that religion is unimportant. But, for Glenn, schools that avoid a clear secular perspective are no better. Their agnosticism makes them incoherent. He thinks that public schools are in a double bind. On the one hand, an explicit narrative that undergirds a good school's "ethos" marginalizes "worldview minorities." On the other hand, the continual purging from the curriculum of elements that give meaning and direction to human life harms education. The deep differences in society make education in common schools impossible.

THOMAS LICKONA AND THE CRISIS OF MORAL CONFIDENCE

Thomas Lickona believes that everyone can discover the natural moral law through the use of his or her reason. Lickona's theory of religion holds that the moral law is objective and universal and, by contrast, that religion is nonuniversal. His belief in the universal natural law leads him to believe that the most significant feature of the contemporary situation is a crisis of confidence in the

3. Glenn, *The Myth of the Common Schools*, 3.

existence of objective moral truth. Since he believes that people can exercise moral judgment, apart from religion, he characterizes the current situation as a moral rather than a religious crisis.

Lickona joins Howe, Robertson, and Glenn in indicating that America's founders took moral education for granted. He also joins them in saying that contemporary Americans cannot make such an assumption. He blames this on powerful currents in philosophy and society that have eroded widespread assumptions concerning the existence of objective moral truth that once supported moral education. During the late nineteenth century, moral philosophers discovered that moral values evolve over time, suggesting that moral values are relative. During this same period, empirical psychologists discovered that a person's moral behavior would vary according to the situation. This inconsistency led them to declare that character cannot be formed. Later, in the 1940s, the philosophy of logical positivism grew popular. It drew a sharp distinction between facts and values and taught that only facts are demonstrably true. It taught that values, by contrast, are accidents of personal preference.

The growing pluralism in American society casts additional doubt upon common values. To demonstrate this, Lickona refers to the same study Glenn cites, which found that residential communities do not share a set of dominant community values. The rise of personalism during the 1960s and 1970s celebrated the self as a free individual at the expense of one's relationship with the family, church, and larger community.

According to Lickona, these trends gave birth to a new morality that denies the existence of the universal moral law. This morality is captured in commonly heard aphorisms such as "Look out for number one" and "Do as you damn well please."

Lickona believes that this new morality is contributing to growing immorality in American society. He expresses great concern about the disturbing trends among America's youth: over the past decades teen pregnancy rates have doubled, teen suicide rates have tripled, and teen drug use has become widespread. Lifelong teachers confirm these statistics. These trends have not gone unnoticed. In fact, he says, more and more people are coming to realize that American society is in deep moral trouble. People worry that the most basic kinds of moral knowledge are disappearing. He thinks that America ought to be alarmed. America's crisis of moral confidence feeds this crisis of immorality. Although Americans doubt that the new morality is moral, they are also unsure that the immorality is objectively wrong. As a result they are unable to respond.

Lickona says that America's crisis of moral confidence has carried over into the public school. When society came to think of morality as being in flux, relative to the individual, situationally variable, and essentially private, this greatly impacted public education. In response, schools staked out a position of official neutrality on values and retreated from their once central role as moral educators. Public schools gave up explicit moral instruction. They adopted methods and approaches to moral education, such as values clarification advocated by Howe, that do not commit public schools to any specifiable moral content. Public school teachers became paralyzed by the prospect of passing moral judgment. A story he tells, about a teacher who is afraid to contradict students who tell her that shoplifting is okay, is nearly identical to the one Robertson tells. Values clarification approaches, according to Lickona, have reflected America's moral uncertainty and have reinforced it with lessons so vague as to be demoralizing.

Although schools have retreated from an intentional and considered moral education, Lickona notes that they cannot avoid teaching moral lessons:

> As social institutions, they must regulate moral behavior: They require students to obey their teachers, forbid them to fight, punish them for cheating, and so on. They also provide, through the visible actions of teachers and other adults, examples of fairness or unfairness, respect or disrespect, caring attention or the lack of it.[4]

4. Lickona, *Educating for Character*, 9.

He thinks that educators fool themselves if they do not understand that they are already morally educating the young. The mistaken belief that schools can be morally neutral and the failure to critically reflect upon the sorts of moral lessons we want children to learn have contributed to ineffective moral education in public schools.

Lickona views the current situation as an anomaly. Uncertainty over whether America's pluralistic society can agree on the moral values that public schools should teach represents a deviation from what people in every time and place have considered to be the purpose of education. His belief that people share the ability to reason and to discover the universal moral law gives him confidence that public schools can renew moral education.

DAVID PURPEL AND THE CRISIS OF MEANING

David Purpel believes that a sense of the sacred gives rise to religion. This universal sense of the sacredness of life, expressed in particular religions, is an abiding feature of culture that gives shared meaning to common cultural moral commitments. His theory of religion leads him to claim that the most significant feature of the modern situation is the cultural failure of vision in the face of ecological and social disaster.

The world is in crisis, threatened by a host of horrors. He warns, "The dangers of nuclear war, starvation, totalitarianism, and ecological disaster are as real as they are menacing, and not to view them as problems of immense magnitude and consequence is to contribute to their seriousness." The situation is desperate: humanity is "under the gun," "the sky is falling" and "the house is on fire."[5]

---

5. David Purpel, review of *Critical Pedagogy: An Introduction* by Barry Kanpol, in *Educational Studies* 26 (fall 1995), 221. See also David Purpel and Svi Shapiro, *Beyond Liberation and Excellence: Reconstructing the Public Discourse on Education* (Westport, CT: Bergin and Garvey Press, 1995), 135; and David Purpel, review of *Schooling as a Ritual Performance* by Peter McClaren, in *Educational Theory* 38 (winter 1988), 160.

For Purpel, the crisis faced is not merely the external crisis of looming annihilation. An internal crisis is also revealed by the public's despair, failure to notice, and inability to respond. America's moral and spiritual pluralism reflects, among other things, deep confusion in culture about what is truly important and sacred in life.

Purpel views this crisis as preeminently a religious crisis. The threats to human existence and the diseases of the modern human spirit (hedonism, moral aimlessness, despair, cynicism, apathy, and nihilism) are symptomatic of a religious crisis in American culture. American culture needs to produce a new religious discourse, informed by liberation- and creation-centered theologies that will make it possible to envision a new way of living that is meaningful and leads to peace and joy.

He also claims that the same crisis plaguing the larger culture has infected America's public schools. The fact that education does not prepare people to face the threats to human existence or heal the diseases of the spirit demonstrates the spiritual and moral bankruptcy of education. Education suffers the same crisis of meaning as the larger culture. He agrees with the assessments of Glenn and Lickona that schools have tried so hard not to offend that they are morally vacuous. When it comes to moral education the basic strategy of educators has been to keep the schools from standing for anything. To their great discredit, he declares, they have been pretty successful at it.

Purpel views public education more negatively than Glenn and Lickona do. They think that the public schools are merely morally incoherent. Purpel, like Robertson, thinks public schools are worse than that. Robertson claims a spirit of the anti-Christ has swept the schools. Purpel, by contrast, believes the demonic spiritual and moral forces of greed, domination, competition, materialism, and bigotry have captured schools. These forces are at the root of America's political, social, economic, and cultural crises.

In his major work, *The Moral and Spiritual Crisis in Education*, Purpel charges that the response of the mainstream educational reform movement to these crises "borders on being criminal." He says:

> The public is trying to grasp what is fundamental to life, liberty, and the pursuit of happiness and in response educators give them more standardized tests; the culture yearns for meaning and hope, and the schools suggest more homework and a longer school year. The world teeters on the edge of a new holocaust, and our leaders urge us to consider merit pay.[6]

The trifling, petty, weak response of the education establishment testifies to the moral and spiritual bankruptcy of education.

Purpel notes that scholars, critics, and advocates at both ends of the cultural spectrum recognize this bankruptcy. The cultural left correctly identifies the moral failure of public education to address racism, elitism, sexism, and the need to build global consciousness. People like Robertson, despite their strident rhetoric, crude analysis, and insensitive recommendations, correctly identify the spiritual bankruptcy of education.

> The Right has stumbled onto a reality that embarrasses those who like to think of the public schools as divorced from religion. . . . If the Right is wrong, then what *do* the schools stand for? If they are not godless, are they committed to any cosmology? If they reject "secular humanism," when do they do this and on what basis? Can the schools continue their claim to be innocent, nonpolitical, and nonmoral? (To do this would be tantamount to admitting to vacuity.) If the schools are not to operate in a political and moral vacuum, then can they describe and affirm their informing and energizing principles? I do not believe that the school establishment is prepared to meet this challenge because it . . . has only a vague un-

6. David Purpel, *The Moral and Spiritual Crisis in Education*, 42.

derstanding of the language of ideology, religion, and meaning [emphasis Purpel's].[7]

Purpel criticizes Robertson for embracing inequality and social passivity. At the same time, he credits him and other leaders of the religious right for reminding everyone that public education can and must serve some sacred purpose.

THEORIES OF RELIGION AS THEORIES OF PLURALISM

Howe, Glenn, Robertson, Lickona, and Purpel draw on assumptions about human nature in advocating their policies. For these writers, religion features prominently in their anthropological assumptions, so much so that each appeals to a coherent theory of religion. Furthermore, their theories of religion shape their interpretations of the circumstance of pluralism and its effect on public education.

Indeed, their theories of religion function as theories of pluralism. That is, each one's theory of what is universal and particular in religion and morality guides them in interpreting America's pluralism. For example, Howe's denial of objective universal values leads him to characterize America's pluralism as values bewilderment, instead of, say, a crisis of immorality. Pat Robertson's belief that Christianity is universally true leads him to interpret America's pluralism as a decline of Christian truth. Glenn's narrative understanding of religion leads him to believe that America's pluralism reflects deep, unbridgeable differences. Lickona's natural law understanding of religion leads him to characterize America's pluralism as a crisis of moral confidence. Purpel's cultural view of religion leads him to view America's pluralism as a spiritual crisis in this culture.

All believe that America's pluralism has dramatically impacted public education, leading public schools to avoid normative moral and spiritual content. Howe thinks that America's

7. *Ibid.*, 25.

bewildering pluralism makes moral indoctrination ineffective and inappropriate in public schools. Robertson thinks that public education elites have displaced Judeo-Christian values and that this has contributed to the moral decline of American society. Glenn believes that public schools have become incoherent in their attempt to accommodate America's pluralism. Lickona says that America's pluralism has contributed to a crisis of confidence in the normative values that ought to make up a curriculum of moral education. Purpel believes that America's pluralism points to a deep crisis of meaning in this culture that subverts public school moral education.

As compelling as their views may seem, each of these ways of characterizing the situation of public education is incomplete. Public education is undergoing a crisis of confidence that is rooted in a larger crisis of educational responsibility. This larger crisis touches on the values education debate in important ways, including the approach that public schools ought to take to moral education. This crisis needs to be examined in some depth because it bears on the sort of moral education that public schools ought to undertake.

THE CRISIS OF EDUCATIONAL RESPONSIBILITY

Americans increasingly believe that their public schools are failing at their basic task: to educate academically and morally. Signs of this broad-based crisis of confidence in public education abound. These include the growing movement calling for school choice within public systems, charter schools, and vouchers for private schools, including faith-based schools. In addition, Americans are invited to consider home schooling, for-profit schools, church schools, and Internet schools. All these are promoted as alternatives to the notoriously failing public school.

The academic failure of public education is commonly cited as a reason for instituting school choice. Promoters of alternatives to public education report that America's public schools have high dropout rates and high rates of illiteracy, and do poorly

{ TO ORDER

1.800.537.3394 }

THE PILGRIM PRESS

THANK YOU FOR YOUR INTEREST IN BOOKS FROM THE PILGRIM PRESS.

Title of book purchased _____

What comments do you have? _____

Why did you purchase this book? (Check all that apply)

□ Subject   □ Recommendation of a friend   □ Information on cover   □ Gift
□ Author   □ Recommendation of reviewer   □ Appearance of cover   □ Other

If purchased: Bookseller _____ City _____ State _____

I am interested in the following subjects (check all that apply):

□ African American Resources   □ General Interest   □ Religion and Society
□ Biblical Studies   □ Justice and Witness   □ Social Issues
□ Gay/Lesbian/Bisexual/   □ Multicultural/Multiracial   □ Women's Issues
   Transgender   □ Personal Growth/Spirituality □ CURRENT CATALOG

Name _____   Phone _____

Date _____   Fax _____

Address _____   City, State & Zip _____

_____   E-mail address _____

✂

BOOKS AT THE NEXUS OF RELIGION AND CULTURE

THE PILGRIM PRESS

700 Prospect Avenue ▪ Cleveland, Ohio 44115

Phone: 1-800-537-3394 ▪ Fax: 1-216-736-2206

E-mail: pilgrim@ucc.org ▪ Web sites: www.pilgrimpress.com

CALL OUR TOLL-FREE NUMBER, LOG ON TO OUR WEB SITE,
OR VISIT YOUR LOCAL BOOKSTORE.

in international comparisons. They claim that if public schools faced some competition, they would not be so complacent. If parents could choose the schools their children attended, public schools would compete or they would pass away. In any event, they encourage parents to do the right thing and seek an alternative to the public school for their children.

A closer examination of the statistics that are cited to prove the failure of public education reveals that the educational problems of America's public schools are relatively isolated to poorer school districts. True, many suburban schools are mediocre. Anti-intellectualism in America prevents most public and private schools from being all that they could be. Poor inner city schools, however, drag down the aggregate measurements that are used to judge the effectiveness of all public schools. The problems of inner city schools need to be addressed.

Inner city schools perform poorly for many reasons. One is inequality of funding. In most school districts public education is primarily funded through a real estate tax. This method of funding ties public education to the economic well-being of local communities. Shifts in residential patterns and growing inequality in American society have exacerbated the funding gap between wealthy and poorer school districts. In many states wealthy school districts have twice the funding per pupil as poorer school districts. This means that in an area like metropolitan Philadelphia, urban classrooms make do with $35,000 to $45,000 less than their suburban counterparts. The gap between inner city schools and the wealthiest school districts is considerably greater than this.

Tying public school funding to local real estate taxes ensures that the schools with the most needs have the fewest resources. It also means that districts with lower real estate values can levy higher tax rates than wealthy districts and still raise less money. This is unjust. The impact of this lack of resources is there for anyone willing to look. Public schools in poor areas have leaking roofs. They lack textbooks and supplies. They do not have libraries.

Teachers in these schools are poorly paid and often demoralized. These schools bear the curse of a society that does not care.[8]

Many deny this glaring inequality. Neither political party has singled out this issue as cause for national concern or national debate. Most school choice proposals that claim to help children stuck in bad school systems, such as was offered by presidential candidate George W. Bush, completely ignore the problem of unequal and inadequate funding. When confronted with inadequate funding, people often change the conversation to the social problems of those communities.

The sad truth is, funding is not the only challenge that inner city school districts face. To properly understand why urban schools fail, these social problems also must be acknowledged and addressed. Urban schools face a parent deficit. Poor parents, as a group, have a much lower turnout rate for Parent Teacher Organization meetings, school events, and parent-teacher conferences to review a child's progress. Many reasons for this lack of parental support can be offered. Poor parents often find it harder to get off work and lack access to transportation. Many are single parents. Many had negative experiences in school. The general sense of powerlessness felt by many poor parents is compounded by the awareness that they lack the educational background and the social position of the teachers and administrators they must engage on their child's behalf.

Parents play an indispensable role in the education of their children. Parents can read to their children; they can make sure that homework is completed; they can set a tone in their home that says that education is important; they can, by their own example, show their children that education is a worthy pursuit. Church leaders and others need to find a way to help poor par-

---

8. See Jonathan Kozol, *Savage Inequalities: Children in America's Schools* (New York: Crown Publishers, 1991). In the year 2000 the author of this book participated in a project by the Urban-Suburban Partnership in Philadelphia, Pennsylvania, where the task was to build and furnish a library in an urban school that no longer had one.

ents appreciate their educational obligations and equip them for their role as their child's first teacher. They also can find ways to overcome the obstacles of time, class, etc., that impede the interaction of parent and school.

The problems that attend poverty also harm the educational enterprise in poor school districts. Poor nutrition and health care, especially the lack of prenatal care, contribute to learning problems. Poor school districts have a greater percentage of students with learning disabilities and must bear the costs associated with educating them. Drug use, teenage pregnancy, and other disorders associated with poverty also undermine education. An insufficient appreciation of the value of education makes it harder for poor districts to create a community of learning. The upshot is that even if poor districts had the same funding as wealthy districts they could not provide the same quality of education.

The inequality of opportunity institutionalized in America's system of public education is a scandal that cries for redress. Indeed, it is the single most significant civil rights issue of our time. It is directly linked to disparities in educational and job opportunities. It is a leading cause of the high rates of incarceration. It contributes to racist assumptions about the competency of persons of color. It fuels a flight to the suburbs and the destruction of forests and farmland that attends suburban sprawl. It takes an incalculable human toll when the gifts of some go undeveloped and their potential unrealized.

The problems besetting inner city public education must be fought on two fronts. Greater funding equality must be sought as a basic right under the Constitution. At the same time, religious, community, and political leaders must pay much more serious attention than they have in the past to the negative moral and cultural patterns that subvert education in poor school districts.

For this to happen we need a renewed appreciation that all adults have at least some responsibility for all children. Here we faces a troubling trend. Public education in America is undermined by a declining sense of obligation that Americans feel towards one another. It is difficult to accurately measure how much and in what ways this sense of responsibility has declined, but many have noted that Americans are losing a sense of obligation to the common good. Robert Putnam, for example, says that by practically every measure—voting, newspaper readership, PTO attendance, and religious affiliation—civic engagement has declined. He attributes this decline to the passing of "the great generation" whose strong sense of public responsibility was forged in World War II. The moral sensibilities of this generation inclined them to look at the larger picture and to be involved.[9]

The decline of civic obligation is particularly corrosive for public education. This is because education can be viewed as either a common or a competitive good.[10] The benefits of a well-educated public accrue to everyone. At the same time, an individual personally benefits when the education of that individual or that individual's children surpasses that of the neighbors. As a sense of responsibility for public education has waned, people increasingly regard education as a consumption item and turn to market solutions to resolve public education's problems. This shift in viewpoint subverts the hard work of improving failing or mediocre schools and school districts. It even sanctions a withdrawal from public education altogether. Although Glenn is the exception in this regard, what is most chilling about many school choice proposals is the way they justify withdrawing from the project of educating everyone. Many outside of the inner city have little sense of obligation toward inner city students. They are someone else's kids. Those schools are someone else's problem.

The problems of public education reflect a larger crisis of responsibility in American society. Each person has an obligation to play a role in each child's education. Roles may differ as a par-

9. Robert D. Putnam, *Bowling Alone: The Collapse and Revival of American Community* (New York: Simon and Schuster, 2000).
10. Mickey Kaus, *The End of Equality* (New York: Basic Books, 1992), 108.

ent, as a member of a religious community, or as a citizen. All are called to take part in the great project of every civilization—in the education and nurture of the next generation.

One of the ways people should be equipped to carry out their moral obligation is through a program of civic education in public schools. I think it more than coincidence that Americans are facing a declining sense of public obligation at this time, just when the people who went through values clarification are becoming parents. These are the adults who as students were told that they are under no objective moral duty. It should not be surprising that these parents sense little obligation toward others. Likewise, it should not be surprising that they view education as a competitive instead of a common good. Neither should it be surprising that they feel little outrage at the injustice of the current state of public education in America. For that matter, it should not be surprising that they, as a group, have not done a particularly good job at fulfilling their educational responsibilities toward their own children.

The problems facing public education reflect this larger crisis of responsibility. Americans need to put away fantasies that tinkering around the edges of public education will fix what is wrong in society. Furthermore, they must not let vouchers or school choice distract them from the larger structural problems facing troubled inner city schools. They must not suppose that vouchers or school choice will solve the problems of parental and societal responsibility.

It seems remarkable that each writer can note the pluralism of this time and yet draw such different conclusions as to its significance. This is because the manner in which people view the situation facing public schools is not a raw reading of the data but an interpretation that is shaped by anthropological assumptions, moral values, and loyalties. This book contends that people draw different conclusions about the meaning of pluralism for public education because they hold different theories of religion. People also understand the significance of America's pluralism and its impact on public education differently because they hold different conceptions of what moral education requires. To better understand the values education debate, the normative conceptions of education that people draw upon in arguing for one proposal or another will now be examined.

5 | MAKING GOOD PEOPLE

ost people agree that we cannot leave children on their
own and expect them to grow up to be moral. It is more
difficult to obtain agreement on how adults, teachers,
and parents should go about making a good person.
How is character formed? What role do normative moral values
play in this process? Is religion necessary for moral behavior?
How assertive should teachers be in seeking to form the attitudes
and behavior of their students? How much do students have to
discover and decide for themselves?

Agreement is even more difficult to attain when it comes to
deciding how public schools should go about making good people.
Hardly anyone thinks that public schools or teachers should indoctrinate their students. But what counts as indoctrination? Some
define indoctrination as teaching religious precepts. Others define
indoctrination as upholding normative moral values. Still others
believe that schools cannot teach history, science, and social studies
without indoctrinating students.

As previously stated, moral reasoning reflects the interaction of
four elements: anthropological assumptions, situational analysis,
moral norms, and loyalties. We have examined the anthropological
assumptions of Howe, Robertson, Glenn, Lickona, and Purpel that
are inherent in the proposals they each advance. Each proposal
presents a unique way of looking at religion in human life, and each

reflects different theories of religion that influence the interpretation of the situation. Each view of religion and human nature functions as a theory of pluralism that shapes its proponent's understanding of America's pluralism and its impact on public education. But how do their theories of religion influence the third element of moral reasoning, namely, moral norms?

Moral norms are the guidelines—the "dos" and "don'ts"—that people appeal to when advocating a policy. Some connect doing the good to following a set of rules. (This is termed *deontological*, from the Greek, which means "it is necessary that.") Others connect doing the good with the outcomes achieved. (This is termed *teleological*, from the Greek, which means "from the goal or end.") Still others appeal to virtue, or character ethics. Sometimes people appeal to simple maxims, such as the golden rule (still rule based, or deontological). Other times they appeal to enduring values such as justice (still outcome based, or teleological). More than a few appeal to more developed and complex norms, such as professional standards of conduct or Roman Catholic social teaching. Moral norms are inherent in normative conceptions of education.

A normative conception of education answers such question as: What is education? What are its purposes? What should be taught? How should one teach? Who should decide?[1] Normative conceptions of education are normative in that they are offered as guides in the task of education, including moral education.

The normative conceptions of education to which Howe, Robertson, Glenn, Lickona, and Purpel appeal in making a case for their policies are indelibly shaped by their theories of religion. Laying bare the differences among their normative conceptions of education prepares the way to consider the task of education from a more holistic perspective. It also prepares the way for ex-

---

1. See Adrian M. Dupuis for the normative educational questions in his book *Philosophy of Education in Historical Perspective* (New York: University Press of America, 1985), 8.

ploring their loyalties and how their policies derive from their theories of religion.

LELAND HOWE AND PERSONALIZING EDUCATION

Howe considers education to be a student-centered process. He claims that the aim of education is to help students become better functioning human beings. He says that intellectual development or the transmission of subject matter should not define education. It should not be thought that the goal of education is instruction, or covering the curriculum, or higher test scores. The purpose of education is the personal growth of the students.

Personal growth happens as students construct systems of values and meaning. Teachers do not deposit information, knowledge, and values in student's minds as in a bank. Rather, teachers guide students as they try to make sense of the world and decide what is important. Education, according to Howe, requires students to make choices.

This means that the most significant element in education is the student: his or her concerns, interests, and goals. Students, he points out, will not learn unless they appreciate the importance of education for their lives. To promote the growth and development of students, Howe recommends "personalizing education." By this he means that teachers should facilitate personal growth in every area of a student's life—physical, intellectual, emotional, social, and moral. He says that teachers can personalize education by helping students set goals that will bring them satisfaction and meaning. They can personalize education by discovering what students value and want to learn.

This last element is especially important for Howe. To illustrate this point, he gives the example of a girl named Julie who had been disengaged from the educational process and experienced academic failure but recently had found new motivation and success. The difference was that "instead of being told what, when, and how she had to learn, Julie was encouraged to discover herself, explore values and her goals in life, decide what things she needed to learn, and learn them in ways that were meaning-ful to her. She began working on projects that she was interested in and at which she could succeed."[2]

As this indicates, Howe believes that the agent who should control the educational process (and who ultimately does control it, whether parents or teachers like it or not) is not the teacher, or the school, but the student. Only when students decide what is worth knowing and see the relevance of learning for their goals will they invest themselves in the hard work that education re-quires. This unavoidable fact of education is why education must be a student-centered process. The teacher's task is to help stu-dents assume responsibility for their own education.

Howe's understanding of education has important implica-tions for moral education. The purpose of moral education, he declares, is not to create blind rule-followers, but to help students become better decision-makers. The goal is not to teach a set of moral values, but to form reflective people who are well practiced at making good choices. Moral education involves teaching the valuing process and encouraging students to choose, prize, and act on their own freely chosen values.

Howe's constructivist theory of religion influences his nor-mative conception of education. His belief that no set of values is universal reinforces his view that setting forth normative values is a "don't" of education. When teachers imply, even by standing at the head of the class or by moderating discussion, that some val-ues are better than others, they are imposing values on students and engaging in the evil of indoctrination. If teachers give an im-pression that they know the best values, students will not feel free to choose their own values.

Furthermore, Howe's belief that everyone constructs systems of meaning and morality supports the "do" in his normative con-ception of education. His procedural definition of character—as

2. Leland and Mary Martha Howe, *Personalizing Education: Values Clarification and Beyond* (New York: Hart Publishing, 1975) 23.

being good at making choices—reinforces his normative conception of moral education as teaching a valuing process. Since he does not define character by normative virtues or moral rules, he is confident that teachers can morally educate without espousing normative values. To do this they must create a safe atmosphere in which students can choose their own values. They can create a climate of caring and respect in their classrooms by accepting all viewpoints as having equal value and by taking the role of a coseeker in the search for the best values. Teachers should see themselves as friends instead of experts, helpers instead of authorities, and resource persons instead of founts of information and knowledge. His belief that each individual constructs a personal value system makes him confident that teachers can play an important role in developing the important human capacity of moral choice.

ROBERTSON AND TRANSMITTING A HERITAGE

Given that he is not an educational theorist, it is not surprising that Robertson's conception of education is less well developed than others in this book. He describes education as passing on a spiritual and moral heritage. He notes that the classic aims of education involve developing the mental and moral capacities of students. Schools need to teach students to think and to instruct them in the facts and skills that will help them to negotiate life. Teachers also need to instruct students in the moral standards that will help them keep everything in proper perspective. Robertson claims that these standards are expressed in the heritage of a nation, culture, or civilization.

In contrast to Howe, Robertson views education as imparting specific intellectual and moral material to students. If students don't get it—that is, the curriculum content—then they have not learned. Robertson believes that America's public schools are failing precisely because students aren't getting it.

Not surprisingly, Robertson defines moral education as imparting moral content. In contrast to Howe, who believes that students must choose their own values, Robertson believes that students are incapable of choosing values unless they know good values. Students need standards to determine whether something is good and worth choosing. Students who do not know the moral codes and rules lack the tools to make up their minds. Students cannot discover these standards on their own. Someone must teach them.

Robertson acknowledges that the state has important educational responsibilities. These include: ensuring general literacy, establishing public schools, upholding educational standards, and enforcing truancy laws. According to Robertson, however, well-placed educational elites go beyond this and act as if children belong to the state. He disagrees with this, declaring that parents, not the state, have primary responsibility for their children's education. Compared with parents, he says, state bureaucracy is "unnatural and ineffective." Furthermore, God gives children to parents, not the state. Accordingly, parents should ultimately control their child's education.

Robertson's theory of religion shapes his normative conception of education. His belief that humanity cannot find the truth apart from revelation correlates with the "do" of moral education, which is to teach students that they are responsible to God. Students, like the rest of humankind, cannot find the truth by themselves. Teachers must teach them. On this basis, he argues that prayer, Bible reading, the Ten Commandments, and other religious principles in America's national and cultural heritage are necessary ingredients of moral education.

His belief that Christianity is true, whether or not people accept it, leads him to deny that any other standard of truth is suitable to serve as the substance of the curriculum. Secular standards, atheistic standards, communist standards, and humanistic standards place human beings at the center of the universe. They undercut the sacrifices that moral living requires by making humans the measure of all things, by debasing humans to the level of animals, and by viewing life as meaningless. Because they cannot provide adequate moral guidance, these other perspectives constitute the "don't" in his normative conception of education. From Robertson's perspective, the greatest favor that can be done for students is to teach them the truth.

GLENN ON EDUCATION AS HUMAN FORMATION

Glenn defines education as forming persons according to a religious narrative. He does not conclude that everything schools do is religious, but draws a distinction between education and instruction. Instruction, he says, differs from education in scope and purpose. The purpose of instruction is limited to teaching skills and information. Education, by contrast, involves the bigger, more ambitious task of shaping character and forming human beings.

He admits that in practice it is hard to distinguish education from instruction, but insists that the distinction is useful. One can instruct someone to drive or to locate Nigeria on a map without immediately appealing to religion. Education, by contrast, involves religious preconceptions. This is true, even if the preconception is that no religious truth exists or that religious truth is unknowable or that all ultimate questions (and, therefore, all worldviews) are insignificant. Schools cannot form human beings without a vision of the world.

For Glenn all education is moral education. Education or, if one prefers, moral education, goes beyond moral instruction. Moral instruction is merely teaching students the commonly accepted rules of behavior. Moral education, like education itself, goes beyond this to form the character of students. Glenn says that schools cannot form persons unless they know the sorts of persons they are trying to form. They cannot know the sorts of persons they want to form unless they have a picture of how the world really is. They cannot have a picture of how the world really is without religion. Glenn does not think that teachers can explain why moral behavior is the better course, especially when it is difficult or requires sacrifice, without appealing to a religious narrative.

According to Glenn, schools that know the sort of persons they are trying to form have a coherent ethos. He defines an ethos as "a set of beliefs about education, about human life and its purposes, and about the good life and greatness of soul that underlie the expressed character of some schools."[3] In the same way that individuals require a religious narrative for meaning, the community called "school" requires a religious narrative for moral meaning. This narrative exercises an unseen but, nevertheless, inexorable influence on the school community. It shapes the unspoken norms and assumed habits that form the invisible culture of a school. It also shapes the visible climate of the school; that is, the observable interaction, order, and atmosphere of the schools. Glenn thinks that the single most important element for the moral formation of students is the school's ethos. Schools that are unclear about the underlying narrative of life will have an incoherent ethos. He claims that this is the trouble with most public schools today.

The influence of Glenn's narrative theory of religion is seen in his normative conception of education. His belief that moral character requires a larger religious narrative for meaning is nearly synonymous with his contention that schools cannot educate without religion. Schools need a religious narrative to know the sort of character they are trying to form. The big "do" in his normative conception of education is the need to create schools that know what sort of persons they are trying to form.

Glenn's belief that secularism is a religious perspective leads him to insist that it is philosophically naïve and unfair to allow secularism to decide what is permissible in public schools. His belief that religious people have no voice in schools with a secular ethos leads him to articulate the most complex division of educational responsibility of any of the authors examined. Unlike

---

3. Charles Leslie Glenn, "Choice and Distinctive Schools," *New Schools, New Communities*, 12, no. 3 (spring 1996), 44. See also Glenn, "School Distinctiveness," *Journal of Education*, 176, no. 2 (1994), 73.

Howe, who thinks that education finally rests on the student, and unlike Robertson, who believes God gives parents ultimate educational control, Glenn identifies three parties that have an interest in public education. These parties are: parents, society, and educators. Each of these, he says, should take a leading role in answering a basic question about schooling. Society should concern itself with the "what" of education and institute guidelines to hold schools accountable. Educators should concern themselves with the "how" of learning. They should concern themselves with pedagogical technique. Parents, he claims, have a particular concern with the "why" of schooling. Since education is forming students in a religious narrative and no universal narrative exists, parents should be able to choose a school whose narrative and ethos is compatible with their own.

LICKONA ON THE TWIN GOALS OF EDUCATION

Lickona tells us that education has always and everywhere had the same two aims: to make students smart and to make them good. Making students smart involves conveying knowledge and developing cognitive thought. Making students good, he declares, goes beyond this to address the affective and volitional aspects of character.

Moral education, he says, must address all dimensions of character so that students know, desire, and do what is right. Specifically, Lickona insists, character education must go beyond the intellectual exercises of moral dilemmas and rational decision-making, to shape the dispositions and attitudes of students. Although Lickona complains that schools aren't intentionally engaging in character education, he also insists that character education is unavoidable. Everything that schools and educators do forms the character of the students. Like Robertson and Glenn, and in contrast to Howe, Lickona does not believe that that teachers or schools can avoid normative moral content. The question is not whether schools should teach values, but which values the schools should teach. Schools and society have a stake in leading students to adopt good values. For this reason, he urges public schools to be intentional about the moral values they wish to convey.

Lickona's theory of religion influences his normative conception of education. His belief that everyone can reason morally and discern the universal moral law without referring to religion supports the "do" in his recommendation, namely, to teach the universal moral law by appealing to the reason of students. It also gives him confidence that schools can forge a moral consensus among the religiously plural public around the moral content of character education.

His view that religion is particular and his identification of religion with the personal faith of the believer reinforces his prohibition against teaching normative religious values in public schools. His belief that religion and morality are separable underlies his assertion that schools should teach the universal moral law without reference to religion.

PURPEL ON EDUCATION AS CULTURAL REPRODUCTION

Purpel appeals to a sophisticated conception of education in arguing that teachers should teach for meaning. Education, he says, has a two-fold relationship with culture. It is both the child and the parent of culture. It is the child of culture in the sense that the culture gives birth to education. As a result, education reflects the dominant values and tendencies of the larger culture. Education is also the parent of culture. Education gives birth to culture. It redefines and transforms a new, forthcoming configuration of that culture. "Education," as he says, often "creates a world."

The parental aspect of the relationship between education and culture is important for Purpel. Public schools, according to him, are a place to redefine and transform cultural values. He calls education a "sacrament" because it has the power to drown out the voices that urge people to buy, consume, and compete, and also to help them hear the divine voice that is calling for the creation of a world of justice and peace.

Glenn says that teachers should have a significant say in deciding "how" the curriculum is taught. Purpel criticizes educators for being preoccupied with the "how" of educational technique. Teachers, he asserts, should see themselves as "tranformative intellectuals." That is, they should see that they are called to address the broken aspects of social and political life. He goes well beyond Glenn in insisting that public school teachers should have a significant, even a primary voice in the "what" and "why" of education.

Purpel's normative view of education has important implications for moral education. If the goal of education is to make a world, the first goal of moral education is to create a good world. Purpel denies that most of what passes for moral education is moral. He accuses Lickona, for example, of promoting immoral complacency. Purpel criticizes Lickona for narrowly focusing on personal immorality and never considering the immorality of political and economic institutions. Purpel says that moral education is not needed; instead we require a moral analysis of America's cultural predicament. Educators must be aware of the corrupt social and political values and structures that permeate society and the public schools. They must also possess an alternative vision of the way that the world should and could be. The best source for such a vision, according to Purpel, is religion.

The cultural dimensions of Purpel's conception of education should not distract from his belief that education forms persons. Education forms persons through the processes of integration, acculturation and socialization. The character-forming dimensions of Purpel's normative view of education are seen in his "educational credo." It urges teachers to work with their students to nurture and develop: (1) wonder and awe, (2) meaning making, (3) an awareness of the oneness of nature and humanity, (4) a cultural mythos, (5) the traditions of democratic principles, and (6) attitudes of outrage and responsibility.[4] Purpel's credo seeks to form students with a disposition to engage the culture. It seeks

4. David Purpel, *The Moral and Spiritual Crisis in Education*, 113-19.

to give students a moral vision that will sustain them in the task of creating a world of love and joy.

Purpel's view of religion as a feature of culture corresponds to his view of education as cultural reproduction. He tells educators not to indoctrinate their students, but defines indoctrination narrowly as teaching the tenants of a particular religion. Robertson, from Purpel's perspective, seeks indoctrination.

At the same time, Purpel's belief that religion is a feature of culture leads him to believe that public schools cannot avoid religious questions. As the child of culture, cultural religion intrudes on public education. As the parent of culture, public education shapes cultural beliefs. Purpel's belief that the culture's religious dimensions encompass and transcend the particularity of religious groups supports the "do" of his normative conception of education. It allows him to regard teachers as prophets entrusted with the task of reforming the culture's moral vision in light of its highest values. It supports his recommendation that educators "narrow the gap of beliefs among [religious] groups" and forge an "overarching framework of meaning for our culture."[5] It informs his counsel that teachers socialize students into a "grand consensual myth" that will guide them in creating a world of justice and peace. His view that religion is a feature of culture reinforces his claim that teachers can do this without raising First Amendment concerns. He denies that teaching the culture's myths, narratives, and traditions is indoctrination. It is the much neglected and needed "do" of moral education.

THEORIES OF RELIGION AND MORAL NORMS

Howe, Robertson, Glenn, Lickona, and Purpel advocate distinctive normative conceptions of education. What they consider universal in their theories of religion directly correlates with the positive guidance, or the "dos" in their normative conceptions of education. Howe urges teachers to help their students construct

5. *Ibid.*, 74.

their own systems of moral meaning by teaching a valuing process. Robertson believes that teachers are obligated to teach students the true faith. Glenn calls for a system that will allow religious communities to form students in a narrative. Lickona urges public schools to teach the universal moral law by appealing to the reason of their students. Purpel recommends that teachers transmit culture's highest moral and spiritual values to students.

Just as these writers derive their positive rules for guidance, their "dos" in moral education, from their theories for religion, they also derive their negative rules, their "don'ts" in moral education, from their theories of religion. All agree that public schools should not engage in indoctrination. Yet each defines indoctrination differently, according to his theory of religion. Howe believes that religious and moral values are as particular as the individuals who construct them. On this ground, he says teachers who tell students that some values are better than others indoctrinate their students. Robertson believes that positions other than Christianity are in error and, thus, rejects them as the substance of the public school curriculum. He bemoans the fact that educational elites are indoctrinating students in false religious beliefs. Glenn believes that narratives are as particular as the communities that tell them. He thinks that it is wrong to impose one's narrative on others through the common school. Lickona thinks that religious values are particular. If public schools were to teach them, that would be indoctrination. Although Purpel thinks that particular religions share a universal sense of the sacred, teachers should not advocate any particular religion when they teach because that would be indoctrination.

MAKING GOOD PEOPLE IN SCHOOL

Each author's normative conception of education has at least some validity. A more adequate normative conception of education will encompass a number of things that these writers seek to uphold.

Howe is certainly correct to view education as a student-centered process, in the sense that teachers work with developing human beings who have their own minds and wills. The purpose of moral education is to help students internalize a set of moral values. We do not want students who suffer value confusion and who have never decided what is important in their lives. Neither do we want them to become moral automatons who thoughtlessly and passively conform to prevailing social norms. We want students to internalize a set of good moral values, to develop the capacity to be morally reflective, and to have the courage to follow their consciences.

This last point is especially important as public education in public schools is considered. Howe is simply wrong to assert that students can only choose their own values if teachers pretend that it does not matter what values they choose. Students do not construct value systems in a vacuum, but in moral communities. Public schools are inevitably one such community that exercises an important formative influence on young people. Everything about the public school teaches. Public schools exist to promote causes that have important moral dimensions, such as universal literacy and the responsibilities of citizenship. History, literature, and science all touch on moral dimensions of life. Public schools uphold unspoken and perhaps unintended norms, such as the example that only women teach in elementary school. They enforce other norms by rewarding some behaviors, such as diligent study, and punishing others, such as cheating.

When the portion of the curriculum that is devoted to explicit moral education is considered, the stake that schools and the public have in forming moral students must be acknowledged. Character cannot be defined procedurally, the way Howe does, apart from moral norms and content. To take an extreme example, no one would be satisfied by the knowledge that Hitler did not suffer values confusion. His values were very clear—but terrible. Teachers and educators cannot be morally agnostic. Students must be helped to internalize good moral values.

EDUCATION IN SCHOOL AND SOCIETY

Having acknowledged that the public school is a community that forms human beings and that it has a stake in helping students internalize good values, it is appropriate to ask what values are to be taught. Before this question is addressed, it must be acknowledged that in American society education (including moral education) occurs in a plurality of institutions. Public schools are not the only community that forms students. Most societies educate children in a host of communities and settings. For Americans these include families, religious communities, for-profit learning centers, music lessons, summer camps, sports leagues, a host of voluntary associations, and an ever-present media. Robertson, Glenn, and Purpel are insufficiently aware of the plurality of educational settings that do (and should) exercise a formative influence on children. The failure to acknowledge the plurality of educational institutions in society leads them to exaggerate the importance of public school for the formation of persons. It leads them to overstate the faults and flaws of public education and gives each inordinate confidence that his proposal will, by itself, solve the problems of education in America.

Robertson, curiously, does not take the church seriously enough. Even if everyone agreed that students ought to be introduced to the true faith, it does not follow that public schools are the place to do so. If Robertson had a fuller appreciation of the diversity of educational institutions that impact the formation of children, he would put greater emphasis on introducing children to the true faith in one's religious community.

A host of reasons that public schools should not teach religion as faith can be offered, beyond the Constitutional reasons that are commonly cited. For example, public schools should not teach religious faith because official establishment of a particular religion corrupts religion. When public schools try to teach religious faith (as opposed to teaching comparative religion), they always deny or dismiss the thick particularities of religion in favor of a thin, "common faith" that no one believes. Teaching a particular religious faith in public schools leads to the religious oppression of nonbelievers and violates the conscience of individuals. Theologian Reinhold Niebuhr, in the only article he wrote on religion and education, adds another rarely mentioned corruption of religion. The assumption that religious faith will be adequately taught in the public school may lead to the sort of religious complacency that is a common problem for churches in Europe.[6] For all these reasons, religious education should be carried out under the auspices of religious, not civil communities.

Glenn is at least partly right that education forms human beings in a narrative. Glenn, however, does not take seriously enough the fact that several communities form students. Each of these communities has a narrative that explains its purpose and supports its norms. Glenn does not adequately distinguish between narratives. Not every narrative is a meta-narrative—that is, a controlling narrative that helps a person make sense of all the other narratives that he or she encounters. Meta-narratives are those told by religious and quasi-religious communities.

Glenn correctly maintains that schools should not be religious or quasireligious communities that seek to form students in a meta-narrative. But it does not follow that public schools should have no narrative. The narrative that underlies the public school should be a national narrative about democracy and the American experiment. Schools should clearly emphasize that the national narrative is a particular narrative about this nation and its self-understanding. Public schools should also make clear why they do not teach religious narratives: not because they are particular in contrast to the national narrative, but because religious narratives are more universal and inclusive of all things, including nations.

Purpel may be correct when he says that education is a site of cultural reproduction, but this is true of every community that

---

6. Reinhold Niebuhr, "Religion and Education, *Religious Education* 48, no. 5 (November–December, 1953), 371–73.

educates, including synagogues, scout troops, and baseball teams. Public schools and educators do bear responsibility for creating a good world, but they do not bear this task alone. If Purpel paid greater attention to the great diversity of culture and cultures in society and paid adequate attention to the plurality of educational institutions in society, he would not lay so much of the burden for culture on the public school.

Lickona does the best job of acknowledging that public schools are merely one of many educational communities that form students. His call for a public conversation to generate a moral consensus that will serve as a basis for explicit moral instruction provides a basis for the values that schools teach. At the same time, it must be asked whether it is reasonable to expect teachers to find adequate moral meaning in reason alone. This solution to the problem of religion and morality in public schools is beautiful in its simplicity. But, finally, it is too simple. This is because Robertson, Glenn, and Purpel are right. People do not reason in the thin air of abstract logic. They reason on models and symbols that refer to the world, many of which have religious histories and overtones. In short, we need to find a way to honor Lickona's stress on reason and a public conversation and Purpel's emphasis on the models and symbols that make sense of the world. Ongoing public conversation about the content of moral education should be encouraged and it should be as thick with models and symbols as reason will allow. It should honor the shared responsibility for public education, and the fact that all have a stake in the content of public school moral education. A thick conversation such as this can form the basis and provide the content for public school moral education.

The normative conceptions of education offered by Howe, Robertson, Glenn, Lickona, and Purpel seek to protect something that they think is important. Howe urges teachers not to indoctrinate their students because they want to protect the student's right to choose his or her own values. Robertson urges Christians to replace humanistic values with traditional Christian values to shore up the foundations of democracy. Glenn recommends a system of government-run school choice to protect the parental right to form the religious beliefs of their children. Lickona wants schools to instruct students in moral values to improve the moral tone of society. Purpel urges teachers to teach for meaning in order to make a better world. Each of their normative conceptions of education, like their policies themselves, serves a loyalty or cause. It is time to now examine their loyalties in greater depth.

6 | RELIGION AND DEMOCRATIC CONVERSATION

W hat loyalty does each writer call upon in advocating his policy and how does his loyalty relate to his theory of religion? A loyalty is the person, institution, or cause that a policy is intended to serve. Loyalties are proximate (close or lesser) goods and should be distinguished from an ultimate good. For example, a Christian may understand that he or she ought to give generously as a form of service to God as the ultimate good. An individual might also understand that a lesser but still central loyalty is owed to the church and thus direct a significant portion of his or her generosity to support the church's work. In so doing, a Christian should be aware of the danger of making an idol of the church. That would happen if the Christian's loyalty to the church eclipsed the loyalty that is owed to God. In the following analysis the proximate loyalty that each author's policy serves will be featured.

Determining a loyalty frequently takes some sleuthing. It is often the hardest of the moral base points to discern. Sometimes the loyalty is assumed and goes unstated. In such cases one must look at the way in which the espoused policy is deemed superior to the status quo and other possible policies.

A loyalty also can be difficult to discern because people will recommend a policy on behalf of a constellation of goods. For example, a person may recommend a policy for public school moral education because it benefits students, society, and the cause of education. When this happens the chief good must be identified; that is, the good that receives the most weight and that lies at the center of the constellation of goods that are advanced by the policy.

Frequently rhetoric obscures the loyalty that a policy is really intended to serve. People regularly cloak an unpopular policy and its true loyalty in the name of a more popular loyalty. For example, in the radio address President George W. Bush made celebrating the passage of his tax cut in 2001, he claimed that it was a good thing because it contained a provision that would make the child tax credit partially refundable. This provision pays rebates to poor parents who pay no income tax. Singling out this miniscule provision that he had originally opposed and then lobbied hard to remove, masked the true loyalty his policy served. The lion's share of the tax cut went to the wealthy; the focus of his true central, but cloaked, loyalty. He lobbied forcefully to reduce taxes for the wealthy. Yet, curiously, this benefit, which formed the overwhelming majority of the cut, went unmentioned in this radio address. When Bill Clinton was president, he did the same thing. For example, he claimed that Africa would figure more centrally in his foreign policy and that he would not tolerate genocide in Africa. Despite this, his administration covered up evidence that mass slaughter was taking place in Rwanda and Sierra Leone. All of this is to say that a person's stated reasons for selling a policy may differ from that person's fundamental loyalties for conceiving that policy. One must read carefully between the lines to discern the true loyalty a policy is intended to serve.

Finally, determining a loyalty takes detective work because the person, institution, or cause that a policy serves is always viewed in a particular way. That is the reason people can claim that conflicting policies best serve the same cause. For example, some people say that women ought to stay home with their children for the benefit of the family. Others argue for federal day care to help families. Both arguments are loyal to the family, but hold a different view of what constitutes "the good family."

HOWE AND THE RIGHT TO CHOOSE

Howe advocates his policy in the name of several purposes. He claims that values clarification strategies will further the cause of education. By engaging the interests and concerns of students, it promises to create a positive atmosphere in the classroom. Values clarification, he assures his readers, will make even foreign language palatable to students.[1]

Howe also claims that values clarification will secure a society of productive and responsible adults. It will solve the problem of values confusion that afflicts the nation's youth and help them lead socially productive lives. That is why he believes that moral education should be a responsibility of the public school. The loyalty that stands at the center of his proposal, however, is the student's right to choose his or her own values. His proposal corrects supposed problems with the moral indoctrination approach, namely, that it violates the rights of students and their parents.

Howe's theory of religion holds that all humans possess an ability to construct a system of values, but that no universal religious or spiritual values are available. This influences the way he views the rights of students. Suppose, for example, he changed his theory of religion to a position closer to Lickona's—that some moral values are universal, in the sense that they obligate everyone. Then he would urge teachers to help students construct systems of values that include these universal moral values. Instead, he dismisses teaching normative values as indoctrination. He rejects it because it violates something he views as universally human, namely, the right of every person to construct his or her own value system.

1. David E. Wolfe and Leland W. Howe, "Personalizing Foreign Language Instruction," *Foreign Language Instruction Annals* 7, no. 1 (October 1973), 81.

ROBERTSON AND THE NATIONAL GOOD

Robertson appeals to the good of the nation in making a case for reestablishing biblical moral codes and spiritual values in public schools. In a typical expression of this loyalty, he says, "Unless we can get a firm grip on the ethical moorings of this country and stop its slide down the slippery slope of moral relativity and social decay, our entire culture will soon find itself on a high-speed ride to chaos and anarchy."[2]

Robertson declares that true religion is the cornerstone of democracy. When people do not understand that they are accountable to God, they lead immoral lives. When large numbers of people are immoral, the law must step in and impose order on the chaos. When this happens, people lose freedom. That is why humanistic value systems, such as those promoted by education elites, always end up destroying freedom. On these grounds, Robertson calls for Christians to tear down the liberals' "makeshift wall of separation between church and state" and to restore the values of the Judeo-Christian tradition that are the foundations of democracy.

Robertson's theory of religion influences his view of the national good. He assumes a necessary connection between the welfare of the nation and the universally true religion. Robertson says that God is jealous and that nations that wander after false gods incur a penalty. God blesses faithful, obedient nations. Nations that forsake God and violate God's commands invite God's wrath. He claims that recent hurricanes and earthquakes portend signs of trouble ahead. Robertson reminds readers that God did not spare the chosen people. Unless America repents, he says, God will not spare this nation either.

GLENN AND THE RIGHTS OF PARENTS

Glenn is also clear about the loyalty that school choice serves. It serves the rights of parents to transmit their religious beliefs to

---

2. Robertson, *The Turning Tide*, 244.

their children. This is the great flaw of common schooling that his proposal is designed to cure. The fact that his proposal will also renew moral education is an important but corollary benefit. The true purpose of his proposal is to advance the rights of parents to raise their children up in their religion.

Glenn's theory of religion decisively shapes the way he views the rights of parents. If Glenn were to change his theory of religion and hold that something was universal in the realm of meaning and morality, this would alter his view of the rights of parents. For example, if Glenn thought, as Robertson, that teaching the universally true narrative was an important social good, then his view of parental rights would be greatly limited.

Everyone, he believes, is formed in a narrative, but no universal narratives exist. Thus, the right to form the religious convictions of one's children is a matter of religious freedom. It is part and parcel with the right to practice one's religion according to the dictates of one's conscience. Put negatively, it is as wrong to alienate a child from his or her parent's religious beliefs, as it is to force a person to change religion. From Glenn's perspective, education is forming a person in a narrative. It follows that common schooling abrogates the religious freedom of parents. He appeals to the *Universal Declaration of Human Rights* and the *International Covenant on Economic, Social and Cultural Rights*, both of which support the rights of parents to choose schools that are in accord with their religious convictions. Glenn claims that the current system of public education discriminates against the poor by placing an impossible financial burden on parents who wish to exercise their religious right.

LICKONA AND DEMOCRATIC COOPERATION

Lickona says that his proposal will serve a constellation of loyalties. It will help individual students by guiding them in living more productive lives. It will further the cause of education by creating respectful, productive classrooms. It will raise the moral tone of society and further democracy. This last goal is the central loyalty in Lickona's proposal. Lickona views democracy as a form of social cooperation that can only succeed if it can overcome the individualism it also fosters. Although each writer claims that his proposal will improve the moral tone of society, in no other proposal does this loyalty figure so centrally. Lickona declares that in poll after poll a majority of people say that America is experiencing moral decline. He cites numerous statistics that suggest that they are right and offers his proposal as a curative. Educating for character, he promises, will channel individualism into community.

Lickona's theory of religion shapes his view of the loyalty. Suppose he believed, as Robertson does, that a universal moral law is objectively true and that true religion gives true moral guidance, even if many people do not seem to know it. Then Lickona's approach to the moral health of American society would alter significantly. The health of American society would not just be cast in moral terms, but also in spiritual terms.

PURPEL AND CREATING A WORLD

Education, for Purpel, has no other purpose than creating a world of peace, love, justice, and joy. This cause is his loyalty. Since education forms culture, the primary vocation of educators is not to improve instruction, or teach the curriculum, or provide an orderly school. The primary duty of educators is to engage in the struggle to create a world without hunger and want: a world where everyone is safe and treasured. The vision and cause of a just and peaceful world is the loyalty by which he judges everything in education. "I am dedicated to moral commitment and to meaning before anything else, before critical thinking, before creativity, before reading, before great literature and art, even before Einstein's theory of relativity. I see the value of education to the extent that it serves the good."[3]

3. David Purpel, *Moral Outrage in Education* (New York: Peter Lang Publishing, 1999), 248.

The trouble, according to Purpel, is that most educators never consider this. He says that a truly moral program of education would foster outrage at how American culture values success, materialism, and individual achievement at the expense of community. It would work to create a better world.

If Purpel changed his theory of religion and said, with Glenn, that religious narratives are incommensurable and denied the possibility of shared meaning, he could no longer view religion as a key to bringing about cultural change. As it is, he believes that American culture possesses religious dimensions that can be shared by all. This means that educators can take part in the task of creating a "grand consensual myth" that will give energy and direction in challenging the status quo.

RELIGION AND DEMOCRATIC CONVERSATION

As the forgoing analysis shows, theories of religion play a significant role in the values education debate. How religion is defined will determine what is thought to be permissible in public education. This is seen in the Supreme Court's effort to define religion. In decisions concerning public education, the Court has defined religion narrowly as cult, symbol, and ritual, as something "inviolably private," and "individual experience," and a product of "choice." By contrast, in cases involving conscientious objection to military service, the Court has employed a much more expansive definition of religion. In these cases it has defined religion as a feature of humanity, so that everyone, even if they do not consider themselves religious in a theistic sense, may be a religious conscientious objector. Proponents of government support to religious schools argue that if the Court were consistent and employed the same broad definition or religion to cases concerning public education, it could no longer regard secular public schools as religiously neutral. Leaving aside the fact that legal terms may reasonably have different meanings in different contexts, they are right. The way in which religion is defined will determine what is permissible in public schools or whether common schooling is permissible at all.

Thus, differences between theories of religion drive much of the controversy over the proper role and place of religion in public life. It is apparent that so long as people mean different things by religion they will not agree on the proper role of religion in public life, including public schools.

Religion is a practical problem for public education, however public education is structured. People cannot be true to the First Amendment if they do not know what is and is not religion. Something has to count. School administrators, parents, teachers, public officials, and others need a theory of religion to guide them in determining what is permissible in public schools.

In this connection, it is important to confront the specious argument that a system of school choice will neatly resolve this problem. Unless the plan is to simply give money to parents and let a thousand flowers (and noxious weeds) bloom, school choice will not solve anything. The truth is that even a system of school choice must discriminate against some faith-based approaches to education because they violate important public goods. Racist schools or schools that advocate the violent overthrow of the government will not and should not receive tax money, even if they derive their teachings from religion. They should be denied funds on substantive grounds, because their views fall outside the limits of what is acceptable in society.

Therefore we must move beyond analyzing the role that theories of religion play in the values education debate to inquire as to which definition of religion best serves as a normative guide for a public discussion of the implicit and explicit substance of public school moral education. It has been claimed here that the content of moral education should be grounded in an ongoing public dialogue. What should such a dialogue look like? What should be its rules?

First, participants in this dialogue need to appreciate that this dialogue does not take place in the abstract; it takes place in this particular nation. That is to say, participants in this dialogue should recognize that it is a dialogue with and in the American tradition. Participants should appreciate the particularity of this tradition and view the purpose of this dialogue to extend and perfect this tradition, especially as it relates to public education. It should be common for participants to retrieve aspects of this tradition, such as founding documents and classic statements of this tradition, as well as religious statements and movements that shaped the American experience.

Second, participants in this dialogue should recognize that this tradition has been and continues to be flawed. American history includes glorious moments, such as the preservation of the Union in the Civil War, the ending of legal discrimination in the civil rights movement, and the Marshall Plan to rebuild Europe and Japan. But it also includes slavery, the disenfranchisement of women, the destruction of Native Americans, the exclusion of minorities, and environmental degradation. Participants should recognize the need for ongoing dialogue to perfect the union. They should hold a posture of openness and not preempt the dialogue with prior and nonnegotiable opinion.

Participants in this dialogue should be allowed to bring their religious voices into the dialogue. They should not be forced to use the language of nonreligious "public reason," although they should be willing to clarify their views so that others can understand them.[4] At the same time, they must be willing to listen openly and respectfully to the alternative positions of others. The goal of this dialogue is "thick" agreement between the parties of the dialogue. This agreement can serve as the core of implicit and explicit moral education. With this understanding of public dialogue in mind, it is time to ask about the strengths and weaknesses of each theory of religion discussed earlier, especially as each relates to supporting and sustaining participants in this dialogue.

4. On this point I disagree with John Rawls, *Political Liberalism* (New York: Columbia University Press, 1993).

Leland Howe

The virtue of Howe's constructivist theory of religion is that it is attentive to the need for individuals to create their own meaningful system of moral values in the sense that they must claim values as their own. More than others, Howe is aware of the key role that students play in moral education. Values are never simply transmitted to the next generation as a whole, even though some seem to believe this. In the process of education, religious and moral values are inevitably adopted, adapted, and rejected.

A number of criticisms can be leveled at Howe's theory of religion. One is that it is insufficiently attentive to the social dimensions of human existence. Individuals do not choose values and construct meaning in a vacuum but rather within communities that exhibit and uphold norms. One of the great ironies of human development is the way that individuals can be defined by the values and communities they reject. Public schools inevitably constitute a community of values. In his early writings Howe instructs teachers, in no uncertain terms, not to betray their own value preferences, as this would violate the tenet that students freely choose their own values. In later writings, however, he allows teachers who are uncomfortable with a student's values to push him or her to reconsider them in light of their repercussions.[5] This, of course, brings in moral norms through the back door. The unavoidability of moral norms suggests that public schools should be more intentional and clear about the normative values undergirding the curriculum than Howe suggests.

A second criticism is that Howe's theory of religion cannot support a conversation about the aims of public education. If values are so individual, then public decisions about education have no moral grounding or standing. They are mere assertions of power. Many writers note that values clarification's denial of

---

5. Howard Kirschenbaum, Merrill Harmin, Leland W. Howe, and Sidney B. Simon, eds., "In Defense of Values Clarification," *Phi Delta Kappan* 58, no. 10 (June 1977), 745.

moral norms is at least somewhat nihilistic. This brings one to a point of consistency. Howe's proposal assumes that some values (such as the importance of public education and respecting the right of students to choose their own values) are more universal than his theory of religion suggests.

Pat Robertson

Robertson's theory of religion can be credited with being attentive to the psychology of believing. It would be illogical for one to think that one's beliefs are not true about the world. More than many, he understands that people cannot have the courage of their convictions unless they have some confidence that their convictions conform to the way things really are—that is, to the objective truth of things. Although one must raise serious questions about the way Robertson understands religions other than his own, one can appreciate his attempt to interpret them from within his tradition.

Several criticisms may be leveled at Robertson's proposal and the theory of religion that supports it. The common complaint is that he seeks to impose his moral and religious values on others. It should also be noted that his theory of religion undercuts the sort of conversation that makes public schools possible. For example, he claims that the errors of secular humanism arise from its denial of God and that Hinduism is demonic. Can secular humanists and Hindus have any confidence that they will be allowed any voice in a public conversation on the aims of public education? Robertson's theory of religion cannot sustain a public conversation on the ends and means of public education.

Charles L. Glenn

The virtue of Glenn's philosophy of religion is that it is attentive to the particularity of religious belief. He notes that people who do not deem themselves religious possess prerational beliefs about the world that provide meaning and thus function like a religion. One can also agree with Glenn's assertion that religious narratives shape moral thinking in important, powerful, if complicated, ways. His insistence on the irreducibility of religious narratives makes him sensitive to the ways that public schools discriminate against religious minorities.

The trouble with Glenn's theory of religion is that it overemphasizes the role of religious narratives in providing meaning. Meaning cannot be entirely imbedded in religious narratives because meaning is not just a function of language. For language to be meaningful, it must refer to something besides the other words in the language system. It must name realities that exist in the one world in which all narratives live. The theologian Paul Tillich said that philosophers commonly assume that "the *logos*, the word which grasps and shapes reality, can do so only because reality itself has a *logos* character." Religious ways of knowing are implicitly ontological.[6] If religious language is implicitly ontological, then it is possible to hold a meaningful conversation among people of different religious traditions.

On a practical level, Glenn so collapses moral values into incommensurable narratives that his readers are left to wonder how one can have a meaningful conversation about the more limited but, nevertheless, shared aims of a system of government-run school choice. If his view is accepted, how can public funding be given to Roman Catholic schools that discriminate against women as priests, without also supporting a faith-based, white supremacist school that teaches that people of color are second-class? Glenn's theory of religion provides no basis for distinguishing between these sorts of cases. Distinctions between a Roman Catholic school and a racist school fall apart for the same reason that he says common schooling falls apart—no narrative neutral way is available to adjudicate such cases. The fact is that his theory of religion cannot even sustain a conversation on the limited aims of a system of government-run school choice.

---

6. Paul Tillich, *Systematic Theology*, vol. 1, *Reason and Revelation* (Chicago: University of Chicago Press, 1951), 75.

Thomas Lickona

The appeal of Lickona's philosophy of religion is the clear distinction it draws between morality and religion. His assertion that people of different religious traditions can not only share moral values but that they can share a thin, but nevertheless morally significant, account of those values is essentially correct. This distinction offers a strong foundation for a public conversation among diverse religious groups on the ends and means of public education. His theory of religion is also attractive because it provides clear guidance for what schools can and cannot teach: they can teach morality, but not religion. Finally, his theory of religion is appealing because it seems to fit with the United States' Constitution's assumption that people do not need religion in order to obey the law.

At the same time, Lickona's division between religion and morality is overdrawn. It is true that religion and morality are analytically distinct. That is, they can be studied separately. His assertion that one can base morality on reason alone and that the common moral language is the language of reason sanitized of religious content, however, is misleading. People do not reason in thin air. Rather, they reason through models and symbols, most of which have religious roots. For example, Lickona says that public schools should teach chastity on the grounds of "reason alone." The virtue of chastity, however, did not suddenly materialize. It has a long religious heritage and continues to carry religious overtones. His unwillingness to acknowledge this invites the criticism that he has a "conservative Catholic moral agenda." The same religious background is true of other symbols, from "stewardship" to "Good Samaritan Laws," that he believes ought to appear in a curriculum of moral education. The religious dimensions of public moral reasoning are not limited to symbols and models. Public conversation about morality adjudicates the relative claims of centers of value like the nation, the family, the economy, humanity, and the environment. The trust and loyalty that people place in these centers of value reveals yet another, potentially religious dimension to the public conversation.

All of this is to say that Lickona's greatest strength is also his most crippling weakness. The bright and shining line he draws between universal moral values and particular religious values leads him to be insufficiently attentive to the ways in which religion contributes substantive moral content. As one moves beyond insipid moral generalities into specifics and detail, one must address religious meaning.

Another criticism that may be leveled at Lickona concerns the practical effect of his proposal. Although he envisions a deeply moral conversation on the purposes of education, one wonders whether participants in this conversation must check their religious identities at the door.

His assertion that there can be education for character by appealing to reason alone is more troubling. Some would say that his proposal teaches that religion is unnecessary and irrelevant, since it teaches that although some find religion interesting, others manage perfectly well without it. Other critics would go farther and say that his view establishes a secular outlook in public education. In his most recent writings, he has begun to address these concerns and outline practical ways that teachers can bring religion into the classroom.[7]

David Purpel

Purpel's theory of religion is attentive to the similarities among different religions. One might disagree about the points of correspondence among religions, the extent of the resemblance among religions, and what these similarities mean, but similarities among different religions really do appear to exist. The search for commonality among the religions is akin to humanity's quest for unity and is a pursuit that crosses boundaries of nation, culture, and religion.

---

7. Thomas Lickona, "Religion and Character Education," *Phi Delta Kappan* 80, no. 1 (September 1999).

Furthermore, Purpel's theory of religion is attentive to the religious dimensions of culture. Again, one may quibble about what these dimensions are and their significance, but American society does share symbols and centers of value. These supply a common language and support shared commitments that sustain a dialogue about the common good. One cannot understand American culture, politics, or society unless one appreciates the important role that Christianity played in their formation and recognizes the roles that Judaism and Christianity have played in bringing about social change.

Purpel's theory of religion also has several weaknesses. His claim that all religious narratives constitute a single universal narrative is too sweeping. Although individuals can expect, claim, and even celebrate the many commonalities among religions, one cannot say, as Purpel seems to, that the view of the sacred in all religious traditions is the same or of equal value. It must not be overlooked that each religious narrative offers something unique, particular, and different.

For another thing, it might be asked whether or not America's culture is as unified as he says. In many ways America appears to be less a single culture, than a dizzying, jostling collection of cultures. Furthermore, if someone were to distill America's religious beliefs into a single narrative, what universality could it claim? It would be none of the particular constituent religions that it cannibalizes, but an altogether new narrative that likely bears strong resemblance to the beliefs of the person who constructs it.

The practical implications of Purpel's theory of religion are also troubling. One may ask whether his theory of religion is able to distinguish between passing on the culture and indoctrination. Purpel responds to this criticism by noting that American culture's high regard for religious freedom protects against indoctrination. He says schools can provide additional protection against indoctrination by reducing the power between teacher and student by eliminating grading. Finally, however, he urges teachers to forge ahead because the calamities that will follow inaction are worse than a bit of indoctrination here and there. This last counsel does not comfort and leads one to ask whether it is really the task of public education to renew the religious dimensions of culture, or whether this is better left to religious institutions?

PROSPECTS FOR CONSENSUS

None of the theories of religion that have been examined here presents an entirely satisfactory solution to the practical problem of moral education in public schools. Each theory of religion has weaknesses regarding its ability to support public school moral education. Howe's denial of normative values undercuts the public education enterprise. Robertson dismisses some religious voices as illegitimate and, thus, makes a public conversation on the aims of public education impossible. Glenn's insistence that morality is enmeshed in incommensurable narratives leaves one wondering how a meaningful conversation about even the limited aims of a system of government-run school choice can be held. Lickona's belief that one can ground moral values in reason alone favors secular ways of looking at the world. Purpel's view that religion is a feature of culture is unable to distinguish between transmitting the culture and indoctrination.

Since none of these theories solves the practical problem of religion in public education in an entirely satisfying way, one might wonder whether these different views of religion can be brought together and combined into a more comprehensive theory. On first reflection this does not seem so farfetched. After all, Howe, Robertson, Glenn, Lickona, and Purpel agree that religion has to do with meaning. Can they really be so far apart?

If just the three mediating proposals of Glenn, Lickona and Purpel are placed in dialogue, it can be seen that indeed they really are quite far apart. Each writer holds a critical issue in view and, in light of this issue, is able to critique the views of the other writers. Glenn believes that humans refer to and depend on particular, communally held religious narratives for moral meaning.

From his perspective, Lickona's claim that a universally shared, neutral, nonreligious basis for morality exists reflects the assumptions of the enlightenment narrative. Glenn asserts that this narrative is blind to its own religious presuppositions and marginalizes religious voices, especially the unpopular voices of religious minorities. In a similar vein, Glenn thinks Purpel's claim that America's culture shares a common religious narrative and myths that can ground public school moral education disregards the particularities of these narratives and the religious groups that tell them.

Lickona believes that every religion supports a universal moral law and that everyone can discover this through the use of religiously neutral human reason. He believes that the tests of universalizability and reversibility can provide significant and meaningful nonreligious reasons for moral behavior. He disagrees with Glenn's claim that moral meaning is necessarily embedded in unbridgeable religious narratives. Lickona also takes issue with Purpel's claim that religion shares anything like the same universality as morality.

Purpel believes that all religions share a sense of the sacred and that this shared sense of the sacred can provide common, cultural moral meaning. He considers Glenn's postmodern emphasis on the difference of religious narratives to be dangerous because it undercuts the search for shared, cultural meaning. Purpel does not share Lickona's confidence that reason alone can supply sufficient, compelling, moral meaning for moral education and action.

Howe and Robertson, of course, are no closer than Glenn, Lickona, and Purpel. Howe joins with Glenn, Lickona, and Purpel in rejecting the universality of Robertson's faith because not everyone shares it. But Howe believes that they all make too much of the possibility of shared meaning and worries about how this ratifies programs of indoctrination. Similarly, Robertson joins with Glenn, Lickona, and Purpel in rejecting Howe's view that values have only limited, individual significance. But Robertson thinks that they are all misguided in not upholding the universally true Christian faith.

The differences among the perspectives of the five authors are deep and significant. Each has a view of religion and its relationship with morality that is coherent and comprehensive. Each one's view of religion appears irrefutable from his perspective. None is likely to grant that another's theory of religion offers a more adequate account of the phenomena of human religion. Similarly, none is likely to concede that another's philosophy of religion is more comprehensive than his own.

Furthermore, beyond the arguments that the writers have among themselves, it appears that two or more of these definitions cannot be synthesized into another, more inclusive definition, without losing crucial features of the constituent accounts. If emphasis is placed on the ability to construct personal systems of meaning (Howe), the significance of shared moral meaning recedes. In the same way, if the universal truth of Christian faith is stressed (Robertson), it becomes harder to appreciate the value of humanly constructed meaning, other religious narratives, human reasoning, and civil religion.

If it is emphasized that morality receives meaning from incommensurable, religious narratives (Glenn), the broader view of religion as a single cultural phenomenon retreats. Conversely, if religion is defined as a feature of culture that provides meaning to shared moral commitments (Purpel), it becomes harder to maintain the uniqueness and difference of particular religious narratives. If morality is viewed as having logic and meaning independent from religion (Lickona), the importance of the true faith, particular narratives, and cultural myths for moral meaning, recedes.

The opposite is equally true. If the importance of religion is lifted up, whether as the true religion, or in the necessity of particular narratives or cultural myths for moral meaning, it becomes harder to support the view that morality has significant meaning apart from religion. In summary, a single more inclusive definition of religion that upholds all the crucial features these writers have in view does not seem conceivable within their own parameters.

Yet, it may be that Justice Potter Stewart's observation concerning pornography—that he could not define it, but knew it when he saw it—applies to religion. Or as William Johnson Everett observes: "'Religion' is clearly not a homogeneous phenomenon nor an unequivocal concept. [Religion] is, first of all, an abstraction that focuses on certain common traits in human behavior and thought. As a collection of practices it takes as many forms as there are histories of the groups displaying a 'religion.'"[8] If this is true, then one probably could not expect anything like a comprehensive and exact theory of religion that covers every case. Yet, though each theory may fall short, the practical problem of religion and public education remains. Therefore a theory of religion that answers the First Amendment questions surrounding public education is needed.

8. William Johnson Everett, *Religion, Federalism, and the Struggle for Public Life: Cases from Germany, India, and America* (New York: Oxford University Press, 1997), 100.

7 | EDUCATION AMONG THE SPHERES

Religion is a significant feature of the values education debate. An examination of Howe, Robertson, Glenn, Purpel, and Lickona reveals that their theories of religion provide inadequate guidance through the complex thicket of issues that surround moral education in public schools. Also, their views cannot be synthesized to get a fuller account of religion without compromising the premises of their understandings of religion. Still, the values education debate requires an account of religion that honors the rich complexity of religion in all the fullness of its personal, institutional, and cultural manifestations.

Five theories of religion have been examined and have been found wanting. Can a theory of spheres provide a more adequate description of religion and its role in a pluralistic society? To answer this question, we must define the theory of spheres, paying close attention to the role that religion and education play in the spheres. We must also consider the anthropological assumptions embedded in the theory of spheres and examine how they shape the other elements of moral reasoning used with the other authors in this study. Finally, we must consider how a theory of spheres can guide us in doing the task of public school moral education and in solving the crisis of confidence that afflicts public education.

Many social historians, theologians, and philosophers understand the pluralism of institutions in society in terms of spheres,
associations, orders, or mandates. Theologians such as Abraham
Kuyper and Dietrich Bonhoeffer, among others, refer to spheres
and mandates in their descriptive and normative analysis.[1]
Among contemporary theological ethicists, Max Stackhouse offers a theory of spheres—drawn from Max Weber, Ernst
Troeltsch, James Luther Adams, Walter Wink, and others—that
is helpful for looking at the struggles surrounding religion and
moral education and the crisis of confidence that afflicts
American public education.[2]

Stackhouse claims that five core spheres appear in every society, which he calls principalities: the family, economy, politics,
culture, and religion. He argues that these core spheres develop
in response to a human need. The family exists to provide intimacy and nurture for children and adults. The economy arises to
fulfill human material need for food, shelter, and clothing.
Politics grows out of the need for people to live together. Culture
evolves out of the human need to communicate. Religion develops in response to the human need for meaning and for an ethos
that provides normative guidance to the spheres.

Stackhouse claims that any account of the modern society
must not only consider these five core spheres, but also six derivative spheres, which he calls authorities. He claims that three of
these authorities have developed in the West: law, medicine, and

---

1. See Dietrich Bonhoeffer, *Ethics*, trans. Horton Smith from the German *Ethik.*
(New York: Macmillan, 1955); James D. Bratt, ed., *Abraham Kuyper: A Centennial
Reader* (Grand Rapids: Eerdmans Publishing, 1998); and Michael Walzer, *Spheres
of Justice: A Defense of Pluralism and Equality* (New York: Basic Books, 1983).
2. See Max L. Stackhouse, *Public Theology and Political Economy: Christian Stewardship in Modern Society* (New York: University Press of America, 1991), 163ff. See
also Max L. Stackhouse, "Introduction," in *God and Globalization: Theological Ethics
and the Spheres of Life,* vol. 1, *Religion and the Powers of the Common Life,* ed. Max L.
Stackhouse and Peter J. Paris (Harrisburg, PA: Trinity Press International, 2000);
and Max L. Stackhouse, "Introduction," in *God and Globalization,* vol. 2, *The Spirit
and the Modern Authorities,* ed. Max L. Stackhouse and Don Browning.

education. He sees three new authorities emerging in the current context of globalization: ecology, technology, and charismatic leadership. He defines an authority as a sphere that has carved out space in society where it exercises sovereign control. These derivative spheres cannot exist apart from the core spheres, but in developed civilizations they can achieve sufficient independence from the core spheres so as to exercise *authority* over them. For example, a court of law may remove a child from a dysfunctional home and a politician from office. Similarly, a teacher has the authority to fail the senator's child as easily as anyone else.

No society can long exist without creating some means of dealing with injustice, disease, and ignorance, but not every society addresses these perennial problems in courts, hospitals, or schools. In other societies the core spheres or some other derivation of the core spheres takes on these responsibilities. For example, in some primitive societies medicine is entrusted to a religious shaman. Some Islamic countries have highly developed religious courts to enforce *Shari'a* or Islamic law.

In the West, law, medicine, and teaching have developed into discrete professions. Members of these professions exercise authority as esteemed leaders in addressing justice, health, and education. The professions have institutionalized and consolidated their authority in different ways. One way they have institutionalized their authority is through professional associations. These associations serve a gate-keeping function, guarding entrance to the professions by setting educational requirements, examining aspiring members of the profession against a body of knowledge and in their proficiency of skills, and granting professional accreditation. They also advance the profession by requiring continuing education, maintaining codes of ethics, enforcing professional behavior, lobbying the government and public opinion on behalf of the profession, and addressing the larger causes of justice, health, and education in the society.

The account of the spheres that follows is informed by the Reformed tradition of Christianity and seeks to be faithful to the fullness of the Protestant theology that underlies the theory of spheres used here. It does so, without apology, in order to develop the full voice of this tradition with all its insight and nuance. This presentation is offered in its full theological wrappings in anticipation that people of other religious traditions will discover that it resonates with aspects of their own belief system and in the hope that it will aid their own understanding of this complex problem. Developing the full voice of this tradition will, it is hoped, assuage the doubts, growing in many parts of the Christian church, regarding the wisdom of common schooling.

Understandably, many will wonder whether a theological concept can bring any clarity to debates over the role of religion in an institution that Americans properly view as secular. Some might doubt that a concept developed in the Christian tradition can speak to non-Christians and will question whether such a concept can help a religiously plural society approach the task of moral education in public schools. We can only invite them to judge for themselves.

THE THEORY OF SPHERES

A theory of spheres helps us appreciate that each sphere is a discrete sector, operating by a distinctive spirit. The logic of this spirit is expressed in a cluster of norms, rules, and virtues that is unique to that sphere. We see the uniqueness of the spheres when their interests or claims conflict. For example, the logic of the economy permits the buying and selling of a variety of goods and services. Marketing wives, children, and sex, however, violates the spirit of the family. Again, the logic of the family dictates that people belong to the family by birth or marriage. When a family business faces the prospect of firing a family member, it experiences a crisis of norms. Just as healthy family relationships do not usually involve formal performance reviews and dissolution of family relationships by "firing," healthy business practice usually does not encourage keeping a nonperforming person in a job solely because he or she is the boss's son or daughter.

Although the spheres are distinct, they influence one another. For example, the transition of the American economy from a nineteenth-century agricultural society to a twentieth-century industrial society contributed to a rethinking of gender roles in the family. When women's work moved from the home to the factory, it gave women a public role outside the home. Similarly, the shift in theological thinking that occurred with the sixteenth-century Protestant Reformation led to a significant rethinking and reformation of politics, the family, and the economy. For example, the Holy Roman Empire was both a spiritual and a political entity. The split in the Holy Roman Empire, occasioned by the Protestant Reformation, led to a rethinking of the relationship between secular and spiritual authority. Again, prior to the Protestant Reformation, Western Christians viewed marriage as a sacrament. Protestant theologians, by contrast, came to view marriage variously as an estate, a covenant, and a commonwealth. Each of these views led to different judgments about divorce, annulment, and the rights of women.

Each of the spheres reflects God's creative design as well as the curse of the human fault that theologians call sin. Sin produces corruption and alienation. Commonly, sin is thought of as failing to live up the norms and values of the sphere, as, for example, when a parent abandons a child, or a scientist invents data to support a thesis, or a politician uses political power to help cronies.

Sometimes a sphere will become preoccupied with its own value. This results in the corruption that theologians call idolatry, namely, adoration of a particular sphere at the expense of responsibilities and claims of other spheres. When this happens a sphere will encroach on the others and threaten life. For example, when the lines between religious piety and political power are not observed, religion and politics become corrupt. The twentieth century contained numerous examples of the dangers of the state domination of culture and control of the media, as well as the horrors that result when politics is lodged in a dictator's family.

Other times distortion results when the norms suitable for one sphere are applied in another. For instance, politics is corrupted when politicians buy votes, when nepotism is allowed and "sweetheart contracts" are awarded to family members, and when politics is treated as a media circus for the amusement of television audiences. Similarly, religion is distorted when grace is sold as an indulgence or when televangelists twist religion into entertainment or a for-profit business.

Theologians, social historians, and others note that family, economic, political, cultural, and religious structures vary greatly from civilization to civilization. This is because the core spheres are human constructs, reflecting a particular history of development. Their existence, however, speaks to something immutable in human nature that, according to theologians, has been given by God in creation.

The Family

Family structures and marriage institutions vary greatly across civilizations, from Scottish clans to the modern American nuclear family, from matriarchal cultures to polygamous societies. Yet, every civilization possesses some family structure that provides mutual support, promotes the welfare of children, and channels sexual intimacy into the building up of community. Theologians trace the origin of the family to the biblical story of creation. God observed that it was not good for Adam to be alone. In response, God created Eve and told the couple to be fruitful and multiply. Humans are familial beings.

The Economy

Economies range from simple hunter-gatherer societies to complex industrial civilizations, but every society organizes the labor of the human community to secure the means of production and the distribution of goods and services. Theologically, the economy is rooted in the biblical account of creation when God made humans from dust and charged the first humans to keep the garden. This story reveals God's intention to give humanity life through the biosphere and through their labor. Humans are economic creatures.

Politics

Forms of government vary considerably from civilization to civilization, but, whether it is rule by tribal elder or a modern constitutional democracy, every society must find a way to organize and legitimize the acquisition and exercise of coercive power. Although theological accounts differ, the Reformed theological tradition has viewed the state as an inclusive sphere created by God to facilitate living together. After the fall, God gave the state the additional responsibility of restraining evil and securing relative justice and peace. Humans are political animals.

Culture

Cultural and artistic expression has the capacity to communicate and to shape human experience. Over the course of history the human power of symbolic expression has exploited the communicative potential of every imaginable medium. Viewed theologically, culture is rooted in the *logos* shape of the world. The potential of communication is seen in the creation story when the first human names the animals, just as the limits of culture are suggested by the biblical story of the Tower of Babel. Humans are cultural creatures.

Religion

Religion also varies from tradition to tradition and across civilizations. From prayers invoked at a presidential inauguration, to Rogationtide services that bless the crops in the Church of England, to elaborate and extended Hindu marriage ceremonies, every civilization seeks the blessing of religion on the spheres. Furthermore, people in every society look to religion for a metaphysical-moral vision of the world to provide spiritual and ethical guidance and correction. From the perspective of Reformed

Protestant theology, religion is rooted in God's purpose in creating humans for divine communion. According to theologians, true religion is a response to God's call to the first couple, "Where are you?" Humans are incurably religious.

EDUCATIONAL AUTHORITY

Every society must educate its young, but not every society has developed a discrete institutional sphere of educational authority. In primitive societies the education of children is organically enmeshed in the larger community of adults. Individuals in the community may take on identifiable educational roles, such as storytellers, sages, keepers of the rites of initiation, and adults who teach crafts, cultivation, and husbandry.[3] The West by contrast, has developed distinct, formal, enduring, public educational institutions. Children leave their families and communities and are bussed to school or packed off to the university.[4]

Public education constitutes a discrete entity, a derivative within the sphere of education. This is often not recognized because, as with all spheres, public education is related to other spheres. For example, obvious ties exist between the state and public education. In many localities government officials appoint superintendents and persons to the school board, levy taxes, and determine the school budget. Politicians often seek to control the substance and process of education. Lately, state and federal governments are seeking to control education through testing. But in no locality is the school board also the city council. The mayor is never the superintendent of public education.

Educational professionals operate relatively autonomously from government, parental, and religious supervision. They are given academic freedom, which is relative freedom to inquire and the authority to teach. Despite the fulminations of politicians,

3. Stackhouse and Browning, eds., *The Spirit and the Modern Authorities*, 16.
4. Max L. Stackhouse, *Creeds, Society and Human Rights: A Study in Three Cultures* (Grand Rapids: Eerdmans Publishing, 1984), 90.

the pontifications of education experts, the admonitions from the school board and administration, and the complaints of parents, at some point the teacher will walk into the classroom, close the door and teach. For this reason, it is not accurate to call public schools "government schools," as Glenn and other advocates of school choice do.[5]

Public education, like every sphere, operates by norms intrinsic to its sphere, which guard and advance the educational process. For example, it is commonly acknowledged that a professor's evaluative judgment is likely to become skewed if she or he has sex with a student. Again, education is corrupted if a school is considered a business. Schools that confer degrees in exchange for money are called "diploma mills." To take another example, it is often a great shock when entering students learn that a theological seminary is not a church. The seminary is an educational institution that operates, not by the logic of grace and belonging, but by the logic of educational institutions, including admission requirements, homework, grades, expulsion for academic failure, and the protection of free inquiry.

Identifying public education as a discrete, somewhat autonomous sphere should not blind us to the fact that education goes on in every sphere. If we are going to take adequate stock of the intentional education of our children, we cannot limit our view to any single institution, but must look at the whole society. A more adequate view should look beyond families and public schools. The broader view should take into account Sunday schools, music lessons, ballet lessons, on-the-job training, educational television, public advertising campaigns, YMCAs, libraries,

---

5. James W. Skillen also analyzes public education in terms of spheres. He does not distinguish between core and derivative spheres, however, and so does not acknowledge that education has carved out a sphere of relative institutional and professional autonomy. As a result, he collapses public education into the state and calls public schools, "government schools." He advocates moving education from the state and making it an extension of the family. See Skillen, *Recharging the American Experiment.*

Sylvan Learning Centers, tutoring, sports teams, teen magazines, and a host of voluntary associations such as Girl and Boy Scouts. Businesses, government, law, and medicine play important, if sometimes implicit, educational roles.[6]

From a theological perspective, education serves God's creative purpose to form human beings. Humans are born unfinished. They become adults through a long process of nurture and education. Education forms adults by developing children's talents and interests, by instructing children in important skills, and by teaching them about the world in which they live. Education also serves the moral purpose of forming character and socializing them to participate in the world.

A theology of education teaches that children do not belong to parents (as Robertson and home schoolers maintain), or to the state (as in Plato's *Republic*), or to the public school. Children belong to God. They are born into a society of plural spheres, each of which is called to play an important, but limited role in their nurture and education. God entrusts children to parents, yes, but also to the world. Although parents bear significant responsibility for the education of their children, in no society are they the sole responsible agents. One could argue in fact that adults live well beyond their childbearing and child-rearing years precisely because the education and nurture of children requires the involvement and commitment of people besides parents. The obligation for the education of children weighs upon the whole community. God calls each sphere and every person to play a role in the stewardship of the education of children. In this light, public school teaching is a morally important vocation that serves God's creative and governing purpose to form people who are able to faithfully participate in all spheres of life.[7]

6. William F. May talks about the image of the physician as teacher in *The Physician's Covenant: Images of the Healer in Medical Ethics* (Philadelphia: Westminster Press, 1983).
7. Raymond R. Roberts, "Renewing Public School Teaching as a Christian Vocation," *The Presbyterian Outlook* 170, no. 15 (5 May 1997), 9.

RELIGION AMONG THE SPHERES

Religion has three requisite dimensions. First, all persons are religious in that they have a worldview or, in Glenn's terms, a meta-narrative. Their world view may not be reflective, integrated, or coherent—in fact, it may be that most people are content to live on the surface of things—but everyone must come to some sort of decision about the nature and structure of reality. Even persons who consider themselves nonreligious and who do not participate in a religious community need to make some sort of sense of their lives: their dependence, gratitude, obligations, failures, suffering, and mortality.[8]

Secondly, every civilization has religious institutions that are organized to facilitate religious expression and devotion, cultivate religious belief, teach religious texts and explore the application of religious teachings, and promote its religious vision in the world. The relationship between religious institutions and the rest of society varies considerably from civilization to civilization. In some nations religion is an established feature of the national life, as in Tibet before the Chinese took over. In other nations, such as India, religion is embedded in the family. In the former Soviet Union religious institutions existed on the fringes of society. In America religion is organized into voluntary corporations.[9] When we talk about religion as a sphere, we are first talking about this dimension and these institutions.

The third dimension of religion is the role it plays in a civilization's metaphysical-moral vision. Religion in this sense refers to two related things. On the one hand, it refers to the metaphysical-moral assumptions on which society and its institutions rest. In talking about civilizational religion, it is helpful to distinguish between a religious ethos and explicit theology, a distinc-

8. See James M. Gustafson's discussion of the religious "senses" that arise in response to "others" and the "Other" in *Ethics from a Theocentric Perspective*, vol. 1, *Theology and Ethics* (Chicago: University of Chicago Press, 1981).
9. See Stackhouse, *Creeds, Society and Human Rights*.

tion that Purpel fails to draw. To assert that every civilization has a religious ethos does not imply that everyone or every group in a civilization holds the same beliefs. Indeed, these assumptions are often fiercely disputed. This vision does not exist independently of the thick perception of this vision by individuals and groups. Because it does exist in their perceptions, it shapes public conversation and the ethos of the civilization.[10]

On the other hand, civilizational religion refers to the way that visions of religious institutions and charismatic individuals permeate the spheres to form an ethos—the broadly shared assumptions about the structure of reality and ethical behavior in the spheres.[11] For example, views of property and marriage in religion and the larger culture have shaped and continue to shape an ethos in education that regards plagiarism as a form of intellectual theft and sex between a teacher and a pupil as a violation of the pedagogical relationship. Similarly, academic freedom—the freedom to discuss, question, inquire, and teach—has spiritual roots that may be traced all the way back to the office of prophet in ancient Israel. Although the school ethos is rooted in metaphysical-moral assumptions about life, one cannot conclude from this, as Glenn does, that it constitutes a religion in the institutional sense.

Religious conflict tends to center on the fault lines among these dimensions of religion. The friction between the personal religious dimension and the institutional religious dimension is why people outside a particular religious institution sometimes feel judged by people inside a religious community, and people inside a religious tradition sometimes feel misunderstood by

10. See Michael Walzer, *Thick and Thin: Moral Argument at Home and Abroad* (Notre Dame, IN: University of Notre Dame Press, 1994).

11. For an account of how religion has shaped the ethos in business corporations, see Stackhouse, *Public Theology and Political Economy*, 125–7. For a contemporary proposal for a family ethos that draws on theological categories, see Don S. Browning, Bonnie J. Miller-McLemore, Pamela D. Couture, K. Brynolf Lyon, and Robert M. Franklin, *From Culture Wars to Common Ground: Religion and the American Family Debate* (Louisville: Westminster/John Knox Press, 1997).

those outside of it. It is the reason that religion is taboo in polite conversation. It is also why some people outside religious traditions (and even some people within religious traditions) are uncomfortable with evangelistic efforts.

The fault line between religious institutions and religion in society is also a source of friction. This friction gets played out within the institutions and within the larger society. For example, mainline Protestant churches have been engaged in an internal struggle with how they should respond to a culture that is no longer mainline Protestant.[12] In the larger society friction occurred when non-Christians complained about Franklin Graham's Christian prayer at the presidential inauguration of George W. Bush. This friction also appears in controversies over nativity scenes and prayer in school.

Given this friction, some might wish that religion would go away. Indeed, many find the prospects of a purely secular public discourse appealing because it promises to limit divisive institutional religious language. This is an illusion. Religion will always remain an inevitable feature of civilization, because the spheres cannot, of themselves, provide an adequate basis for their norms. That is why people look outside the spheres for guidance when the spheres become corrupt. For example, Aristotle says that when the legal code is not on one's side, advocates must appeal to a higher "law of nature." When Hitler's totalitarian regime exceeded the boundaries of politics, Dietrich Bonhoeffer appealed to God's ordering of society in the mandates to call for a reordering of society. Religious visions provide a basis for prophetic criticism and correction.

Interestingly, people appeal to a larger metaphysical-moral vision when they think leaders of religious institutions get out of line. For example, some years ago the President of the Southern

12. See Douglas F. Ottati's account of polarization within mainline denominations, *Reforming Protestantism: Christian Commitment in Today's World* (Louisville: Westminster/John Knox Press, 1995).

Baptist Convention claimed that God did not hear the prayers of Jews. People responded by saying, "God is not like that!" The distinction between institutional and civilizational religion is the reason religion (the institution) needs ethics, and ethics (society) needs religion.

THE INEVITABLE SCIENCE

Theology is an inevitable science. This is true, even if it operates from a basis that claims God does not exist. It is the science that evaluates the metaphysical-moral claims that float through society. This theological task is carried out in different ways in different communities.

Obviously it is a task for religious institutions. A public theology that addresses life among the spheres is requisite for theists if they truly believe they are talking about the ultimate Power, the Creator and Governor of the world.[13] The descriptive and normative task of theology begins with Ernst Troeltsch's observation that, "the science of Society cannot create ultimate values and standards from within."[14] Christian theologians, following Paul in Colossians, believe that "all things," including individuals and spheres, are "created through Christ and for Christ, and that Christ is before all things, and that in Christ all things hold together" (Col. 1:16–17). On this basis members of religious institutions seek to extend their theological traditions and promote their theological vision in the broader society. They also enter charitably and openly into broad-ranging conversations with others in the larger community, including social scientists and persons from other religious traditions, about institutions such as

13. See James M. Gustafson, "The Sectarian Temptation: Reflections on Theology, The Church and the University," in *The Catholic Theological Society of America's Proceedings of the Fortieth Annual Convention*, ed. George Kilcourse, vol. 40 (5–8 June 1985), 83–94. See also Max L. Stackhouse, "An Ecumenist's Plea for a Public Theology," in *This World*, no. 8 (spring/summer 1984), 47–89.

14. Ernst Troeltsch, *The Social Teaching of the Christian Churches*, vol. 1 (Louisville: Westminster/John Knox Press, 1992), 24.

public schools, all the while looking to Jesus Christ as their source, norm, and hope.

This suggests a second way that the inevitable theological task is carried out: open conversation among the members of a sphere. Every professional, corporate, familial, and national community has traditions that inform its ethos. These traditions and ethos, as we have noted, rest on deep assumptions about the nature and structure of reality. These structures are often alluded to in foundational documents and in classic statements of the tradition. That is why in chapter 6 it was claimed that a conversation about the content of public school moral education must engage the American tradition.

We are now in a position to assess the anthropological assumptions underlying the theory of spheres. We see that human beings are social creatures who organize their lives in a variety of institutions. These institutions exist because humans are familial, economic, political, cultural, and religious creatures. Education exists in every society, because humans must teach their young.

The theory of spheres assumes that creation has a moral and spiritual order that is somewhat knowable. Fortunately, people commonly recognize the spheres and sense their obligations among the spheres. The theory of spheres denies Lickona's assertion that people apprehend the moral order through reason alone, but recognizes that people will likely sense this order through their affection for their parents, children, coworkers, clients, profession, or country. In fact, it seems to be the case that few people are able to clearly articulate the reason they sense the obligations that weigh upon them.

In relation to public education, the theory of spheres suggests that its existence and ethos rests upon metaphysical-moral assumptions that it cannot secure. In this sense, the theory of spheres shares much with Purpel's cultural view of religion. It differs, however, from Purpel's theory of religion in that it denies that a single culture can be transmitted through one public school. The theory of spheres agrees that public schools have significant responsibility for culture, but insists that this responsibility rests broadly on all of society's spheres.

We have said that a theory of spheres provides a helpful way to understand education in a pluralistic society, the values education debate, and the crisis of confidence in public education. We now examine these in light of the other three elements of moral reasoning.

CRISIS OF THE SPHERES — THE SITUATION

When we look at the situation of public education through the lens of a theory of spheres we see several things. First of all, we gain a sense of perspective about what is really at stake in the debate over moral education. The theory of spheres reveals that the pluralism of our society is not simply a multiplicity of religious and secular viewpoints that vie against one another and must be adjudicated through a common school that bears *sole* responsibility for the moral education of children. Were that the case, public schools would be a zero-sum game, where most are losers. Although some seem to believe that everything is at stake in public education and talk as if all educational responsibility resides in this one institution, this is not the case. The moral formation of young people is accomplished in a plurality of spheres. The moral tone of society emerges from the voices of a thousand different communities and groups. No single institution, not even the public school, bears sole responsibility for the moral well-being of youth and society.

Second, we see a crisis of confidence in public education. The theory of spheres teaches that when people lose their confidence in a sphere, other spheres compensate. When economies falter, governments usually make adjustments. A crisis of confidence in government management in England during the 1980s led Margaret Thatcher to privatize government industries. A loss of confidence in medicine and law has led to the rise of alternative medicine and to mediation and alternative dispute resolution. Regardless of what one thinks of it, Promise Keepers was a religious movement that responded to a crisis of confidence in the family, especially in the role of men.

Currently the same sort of thing is happening in public education. Other spheres are compensating for the real and perceived failures of public education. Families are responding with home schooling. Government is responding with persistent efforts to reform public education. The economic sphere is responding with entrepreneurial schools. Religious institutions are creating new faith-based schools. Most indicative of all are calls to create new educational authorities by restructuring public education through charter schools and vouchers. Public education is in the midst of a crisis of confidence unlike any it has heretofore experienced.

Finally, when we look at education through the lens of the spheres, we see that the problems in public education cannot all be attributed to public schools. Knowing that no sphere exists independently of other spheres leads us to ask why public education is in crisis. The larger picture reveals that developments in other spheres affect the performance of public schools. Chapter 4 described the declining sense of public obligation to the common good and its affect on public education, especially urban public education. Unfortunately, this is not the only negative trend affecting public education.

Harold W. Stevenson and James W. Stigler have compared schooling in China, Taiwan, Japan, and the United States. One of their findings is that differences in school performance can be partially attributed to differences in the family's educational ethos, involvement, and stability. Japanese and Chinese parents are more likely to attribute academic success to hard work, whereas American parents are more likely to attribute academic success to aptitude. American parents were more likely than their Japanese and Chinese counterparts to prize a child's self-esteem over academic success. American children also receive less parental help on homework than their Japanese and Chinese counterparts. One of their most telling findings is that 98 percent of Sendai, Japan, parents and 95 percent of Taipei, Taiwan, parents had bought their fifth-graders a desk. By contrast, only 63 percent of Minneapolis fifth-grade parents had done so. In addition, Stevenson and Stigler observe that difficulties in families have meant that many parents have so many problems of their own that they cannot be deeply concerned about the academic achievement of their children.[15] Many correlate changes in the American family with decline in well-being for children.[16] Undoubtedly, these changes affect whether children come to school well fed, prepared, and ready to learn.

The media have grown tremendously over the course of the twentieth century. Generalizing about the educational contributions of the media is as difficult as finding reasons to feel hopeful about the media's educational content and ethos.[17] To be sure, wonderful television documentaries and children's magazines, such as *Cricket*, have been produced. But most children's and youth television programming values entertainment over educational content. The commercial youth culture marketed to children and teens seems rarely to value education or support any larger obligations among the spheres.

Religion at the end of the twentieth century has become increasingly private and interior. This is how the number of people who claim to believe in God can remain steady or go up, while involvement in worship and Sunday school goes down. This is how interest in spirituality can increase at the same time that involvement in religious institutions that have historically nurtured

15. Harold W. Stevenson and James W. Stigler, *The Learning Gap: Why Our Schools Are Failing and What We Can Learn from Japanese and Chinese Education* (New York: Summit Books, 1992).

16. For a statement of the effects of changes in family structure on the well-being of children, see Sylvia Ann Hewlett, *When the Bough Breaks: The Cost of Neglecting Our Children* (New York: Basic Books, 1991). Her findings have been echoed more recently in Browning, et al., *From Culture to Common Ground*, 31.

17. See Neil Postman, *Amusing Ourselves to Death: Public Discourse in the Age of Show Business* (New York: Penguin Books, 1985).

a disproportionate share of civic leadership and involvement is decreasing. This is how a book called *The Prayer of Jabez* can be a bestseller and people can be unmoved by the plight of urban schools. There has been a loss of moral meaning in American life.[18] This loss affects public education in innumerable ways. It affects the value people place on education. It affects people's sense of vocation among the spheres and obligation toward the common good. We cannot blame this loss of meaning on public education, the way Purpel does. Public schools are not responsible for religious education. No, the renewal of moral meaning is the responsibility of America's religious institutions. Speaking of the Presbyterian context with which this author is most familiar, Presbyterians are long overdue for a spiritual revival that will renew their commitment to God and to faithful participation in life among the spheres.

When we look at public education among the spheres, we see a number of trends that subvert the educational enterprise. Taken together, the declining sense of obligation for public education, educational values and trends in the family, the commercial child and youth culture, and the transformation of American religion indicate an educational crisis among the spheres. Many, if not most, of the problems and failures of public education rest on the larger failures of society. It is ludicrous for Americans to think that vouchers and school choice will save schools apart from a renewal in these spheres.

18. See Douglas V. Porpora, *Landscapes of the Soul: The Loss of Moral Meaning in American Life* (New York: Oxford University Press, 2001). Amanda Porterfield makes the interesting case that Protestantism's emphasis on an individual's relationship with God and its pragmatism has led people to evaluate religion solely on its personal therapeutic qualities. See Porterfield, *The Transformation of American Religion: The Story of a Late Twentieth-Century Awakening* (New York: Oxford University Press, 2001). Her findings are supported by Wade Clark Roof, *Spiritual Marketplace: Baby Boomers and the Remaking of American Religion* (Princeton, NJ: Princeton University Press, 1999).

EDUCATION AMONG THE SPHERES — NORMS

If the aim of education is to form adults who can faithfully participate in all the spheres of life, then a plurality of educational settings is educationally important. They provide alternative settings where children can explore new roles and experience different approaches to learning. A theory of spheres resists limiting a child's education to any single sphere. It opposes making parents solely responsible for their children's education, as it avoids lodging education entirely in the public school. It encourages the development of a complex matrix of institutions that intentionally educate the young, including all the ones we have previously mentioned.

With regard to public education, a theology of spheres guides us towards a stance of modesty in our expectations for public schools. Stated negatively, such a stance shies away from expansive conceptions of the aims of public education and limits the goals of public schools. It welcomes the fact that we live in a complex society with families, religious institutions, and voluntary associations and that each serves unique educational aims and purposes. It is not surprised that weaknesses in other institutions create problems, such as a loss of the sacred in life, but it respects that other institutions are charged with responding to problems associated with their sphere. It remembers that public schools should not teach faith or become surrogate families. It refrains from seeking to solve every social problem through the public school and resists the temptation to make public schools the totality of a child's education.

Stated positively, a stance of modesty toward public education's goals encompasses aims that serve the public good. Historically these purposes have been understood as preparing students for work and for citizenship. In more recent times, these aims have been expanded to include preparing students for further education. Practically, this has meant that the public expects its schools to teach students to read, write, and do computation; to introduce students to the world in which they live, especially to the particularities of American history and the American democratic experiment; and to equip students with the necessary skills to participate in the economy and in the democratic process. Public schools have also been seen as serving noncurricular purposes such as securing social unity and providing equality of opportunity to advance in our society. While the subjects that fill the public school curriculum are the products of particular histories and worldviews and even have religious dimensions, they cannot be immediately reduced to religion.[19]

Regarding moral education, we see that implicit and explicit moral education is inevitable in public schools. Public school moral education has two limits. On the one hand, as Glenn would agree, it needs to respect the religious particularity of students. On the other hand, as Purpel would say, it needs to be as thick with meaning and symbols as possible. The first limit will prevent the public school from becoming a church. The second limit will enable meaningful moral education. Teachers cannot know these limits unless they are informed by a conversation among parents, religious leaders, policy makers, and other interested parties on the content of moral education. In too many school districts, this conversation is sorely lacking, or when it does take place it is triggered by a divisive crisis.

Having said this, we should be under no illusion that the problem of religion and morality and America's public schools is easily solved. It may be that controversies surrounding religion and morality are ingredient to pluralistic democratic societies. If this is the case, they will likely remain a perennial problem for public education.

DEMOCRACY AMONG THE SPHERES — LOYALTY

One might then ask whether we would better off doing away with public schools. A theory of spheres does not automatically

19. For a discussion of the religious roots of science and its rise as an independent institutional sphere, see Robert K. Merton, *The Sociology of Science: Theoretical and Empirical Investigations,* ed. Norman W. Storer (Chicago: University of Chicago Press, 1973).

support a loyalty to the public school. But it does reveal the role that public education plays among the spheres. It helps us see the ways in which public education can be a means to a healthy democratic society: that it ensures universal education and that it brings diverse peoples together in a single institution and teaches them to work together. Especially in a society as pluralistic as America's, public education forces us to have a conversation on the shared values that make up the content of education.

Protestants can and have offered good religious reasons for maintaining a loyalty to public education as an institutional sphere. These include a commitment to a form of spirituality that requires an educated laity to read the Bible, exercise their responsibilities as the priesthood of believers, and worship God with their minds as well as their hearts. The Protestant doctrine of vocation supports universal education to equip everyone to fulfill his or her calling in God's world. These reasons, derived from the Protestant ethos, have parallels with other religions that may be explored in developing the religious context of public education.

The belief that public education is a key to a happy and holy society led the Church to be at the forefront in creating systems of public education. During the Protestant Reformation in Geneva, the same meeting of the General Council that abolished the mass and established the Reformation established compulsory education at public expense.[20] The Protestant churches that followed in Calvin's footsteps were keenly interested in public education. Later, English public education grew out of the Sunday school movement, as an effort to educate children from the slums. In America the first laws providing for public education can be traced back to the "old deluder Satan" laws in Puritan, precolonial Massachusetts that established compulsory public education in every town of fifty families. When public education was established across America, educational leaders were disproportionately

20. W. Fred Graham, *The Constructive Revolutionary: John Calvin and His Socio-Economic Impact* (Atlanta: John Knox Press, 1978), 146.

drawn from the ranks of the Congregational and Presbyterian clergy. During the nineteenth century some Methodist conferences required circuit riders to preach several sermons a year on the virtues of public education.

Throughout American history, public-minded Protestants and others have reaffirmed their loyalty to the public school as a means to improve society. For example, during the 1960s, when segregation and white flight threatened public education, public-minded Protestants, Jews, and others rallied in support of integrated public schools. The question remains to be answered today, whether public-minded Christians and people of other faiths will recommit themselves to public education as a means to secure the blessings of liberty.

WHAT PUBLIC SCHOOLS NEED

American public education has many problems. Unfortunately many of the solutions that have been suggested by America's political leaders will do more harm than good. What public schools need can be provided by a renewal of the spheres. The spheres must recognize their unique responsibilities for *their children*.

Public schools need families that are engaged in the task of education. They need parents who teach their children self-discipline. They need families that read to their children and who take it upon themselves to enrich their children's education by taking them to zoos, libraries, and museums. They need parents who get their children to school ready to learn and who support their children with time and desks when their children come home at night. They need parents who teach their children that education is important and who set an example of lifelong learning. In short, they need parents to take educational responsibility for *their children*.

Public schools need a renewal of public ownership. They need citizens who realize that public education is an important common good, who are outraged to learn that some school districts do not have enough textbooks for every student, and who will lobby for equality of funding. Public schools need parents and adults who will tutor and mentor "at risk" children. In short, public education needs citizens to take educational responsibility for *their children.*

Public schools also need religious institutions to fulfill their educational role. Religious institutions have a prophetic role to play in insisting that every child have an equal opportunity for a high-quality education. They have an evangelistic role in calling people to repent from the path that leads to destruction and calling people to faithfulness in their vocations among the spheres of life. They have a spiritual role to play in lifting up a vision of God that views education and the life of the mind as forms of divine service. They have an educational role in catechizing children and teaching adults in matters of faith. They have a communal role in building a fellowship whose ethos supports family life, work, and citizenship as forms of discipleship. They have a nurturing role to play in renewing public school teaching as a religious vocation. They have a direct role to play in encouraging involvement in public education, in supporting volunteerism in public schools, and in guiding a discussion of the complex issues surrounding public education. In short, public schools need religious institutions to encourage educational responsibility for *all children.*

At the beginning of this book we looked at the perceived failure of public education and the rush to find alternatives. Now, having looked at public education through the theory of the spheres, we see that public education's problems are not isolated to that sphere, but are related to problems in other spheres in society. If we really want to address the problems of public education, we must also seek to renew and reform these spheres. This author believes that the renewal of the spheres must begin with true spiritual renewal.

Whose kids are they? Ultimately and finally, they are God's kids. As we undertake our role as parents, grandparents, uncles, aunts, teachers, citizens, mentors, Sunday school teachers, coaches, music instructors, neighbors, scout leaders, and employers, we should remember that the children are God's kids and give thanks that we can play a role in their education.

BIBLIOGRAPHY

Alley, Robert S. *School Prayer: The Court, the Congress, and the First Amendment.* Buffalo: Prometheus Books, 1994.

Apple, Michael W., and Lois Weis, eds. *Ideology and Practice in Schooling.* Philadelphia: Temple University Press, 1983.

Aristotle. *Nicomachean Ethics.* Trans. Terence Irwin. Indianapolis: Hackett Publishing, 1985.

Barber, Benjamin R. *An Aristocracy of Everyone: The Politics of Education and the Future of America.* New York: Ballantine Books, 1992.

Bates, Stephen L. *Battleground: One Mother's Crusade, the Religious Right, and the Struggle for Control of Our Classrooms.* New York: Poseidon Press, 1993.

Beckley, Harlan. *Passion for Justice: Retrieving the Legacies of Walter Rauschenbusch, John A. Ryan, and Reinhold Neibuhr.* Louisville: Westminster/John Knox Press, 1992.

Bennett, William J. *Our Children and Our Country: Improving America's Schools and Affirming the Common Culture.* New York: Simon and Schuster, 1988.

Bonhoeffer, Dietrich, *Ethics.* Trans. Horton Smith from the German *Ethik.* New York: Macmillan, 1955.

Bratt, James D., ed. *Abraham Kuyper: A Centennial Reader.* Grand Rapids: Eerdmans, 1998.

Broudy, Harry S. "Religious Literacy and The American School." *Religious Education,* 48 (November–December, 1953): 371.

Browning, Don S., Bonnie J. Miller-McLemore, Pamela D. Couture, K. Brynolf Lyon, and Robert M. Franklin. *From Culture Wars to Common Ground: Religion and the American Family Debate.* Louisville: Westminster/John Knox Press, 1997.

Bruner, Jerome. *The Culture of Education.* Cambridge: Harvard University Press, 1996.

Cage, Mary Crystal. "A Controversial Professor Crusades for Character Education." *The Chronicle of Higher Education* 43, no. 28 (1997): A16.

Champlin, Joseph M., with Elizabeth Drotar and Thomas Lickona. "Children's Moral Development and the Sacrament of Reconciliation." In *With Hearts Light as Feathers: The First Reconciliation of Children.* New York: Crossroad Publishing, 1974.

Chubb, John E., and Terry M. Moe. *Politics, Markets, and America's Schools.* Washington, DC: The Brookings Institution, 1990.

Cookson, Peter W., Jr. *School Choice: The Struggle for the Soul of American Education.* New Haven: Yale University Press, 1994.

Cremin, Lawrence. *American Education: The Metropolitan Experience, (1876–1980).* New York: Harper and Row, 1988.

———. *Popular Education and Its Discontents.* New York: Harper and Row, 1990.

Dupuis, Adrian M. *Philosophy of Education in Historical Perspective.* New York: University Press of America, 1985.

Dyck, Arthur J. *On Human Care: An Introduction to Ethics.* Nashville: Abingdon Press, 1980.

Eastland, Terry, ed. *Religious Liberty in the Supreme Court: The Cases that Define the Debate Over Church and State.* Washington, DC: Ethics and Public Policy Center, 1993.

Elias, John L. *Moral Education: Secular and Religious.* Malabar, FL: Robert E. Krieger Publishing, 1989.

Everett, William Johnson. *Religion, Federalism, and the Struggle for Public Life: Cases from Germany, India, and America.* New York: Oxford University Press, 1997.

Finn, Chester. *We Must Take Charge: Our Schools and Our Future.* New York: Free Press, 1991.

Gaddy, Barbara B., William T. Hall, and Robert J. Marzano. *School Wars: Resolving Our Conflicts Over Religion and Values.* San Francisco: Jossey-Bass Publishers, 1996.

Gerson, Michael J. "Public Schools Teach Bible as History: What Role Is There for Jesus and Jeroboam?" *U.S. News and World Report* (12 January 1998): 23–24.

Glenn, Charles Leslie. "Religion and Public Education: Can We Stop the Fighting?" *Reformed Journal* 34, no. 6 (June 1984): 7–16.

———. "Learning from Dutch Education." *Reformed Journal* 34, no. 9 (September 1984): 14–17.

———. "Why Public Schools Don't Listen." *Christianity Today* (20 September 1985): 13–16.

———. "Two Schools in Rotterdam." *Reformed Journal* 35, no. 11 (November 1985): 5–6.

———. "New Challenges: A Civil Rights Agenda for the Public Schools," *Phi Delta Kappan* 67, no. 9 (May 1986): 653–56.

———. "Equal Time for Religion in the Public Schools," *Christian Century* 103 (July 30–August 6, 1986): 668–69.

———. "What Evangelicals Should Expect of Public Schools," *Reformed Journal* 36, no. 9 (September 1986): 14–18.

———. "When Christians Speak Up in Public: Four Biblical Truths Help Us Apply the Faith to Public Activity." *Christianity Today* (5 September 1986): 6–27.

————. "Rich Learning for All Our Children." *Phi Delta Kappan* 68, no. 2 (October 1986): 133–34.

————. "Beyond Liberation: An Agenda for Educational Justice." *Christian Century* 103 (12 November 1986): 1006–8.

————. Review of *Censorship: Evidence of Bias in Our Children's Textbooks,* by Paul C. Vitz. *Christianity Today* (12 December 1986): 56–60.

————. *The Myth of the Common School.* Amherst: University of Massachusetts Press, 1986.

————. "Textbook Controversies: A Disaster for Public Schools?" *Phi Delta Kappan* 68, no. 6 (February 1987): 451–55.

————. "Teachers for Life." *Reformed Journal* 37 (March 1987): 4–6.

————. "Curriculum in the Public Schools: Can Compromise Be Reached?" *Christian Century* 104 (6 May 1987): 441–43.

————. Review of "Public and Private High Schools," by James S. Coleman and Thomas Hoffer. *This World,* no. 19 (fall 1987): 124–26.

————. "The New Common School." *Phi Delta Kappan* 69, no. 4 (December 1987): 290–94.

————. "Molding Citizens." In *Democracy and the Renewal of Public Education,* edited by Richard John Neuhaus. Grand Rapids: Eerdmans Publishing, 1987.

————. "Just Schools for Minority Children." *Phi Delta Kappan* 70, no. 10 (June 1989): 777–79.

————. "Putting School Choice in Place." *Phi Delta Kappan* 71, no. 4 (December 1989): 295–300.

————. Review of *Privatization and Educational Choice,* by Myron Lieberman. *Commonweal* 117 (20 April 1990): 260.

————. "How to Integrate Bilingual Education without Tracking." *Schools Administrator* 47, no. 5 (May 1990): 28–31.

————. "Schools on Purpose." *First Things,* no. 4 (June–July, 1990): 9–11.

————. "Will Boston Be the Proof of the Choice Pudding?" *Educational Leadership* 48, no. 4 (December 1990–January 1991): 41–43.

————. "Controlled Choice in Massachusetts Public Schools." *Public Interest,* no. 103 (spring 1991): 88–105.

————. "America 2000: Fundamental Reforms?" *Equity and Choice* 8, no. 1 (fall 1991): 62–64.

————. "Educating the Children of Immigrants." *Phi Delta Kappan* 73, no. 5 (January 1992): 404–8.

————. "Hairy Men and Smooth Men." *First Things,* no. 22 (April 1992): 12–13.

————. "Do Parents Get the Schools They Choose?" *Equity and Choice* 9, no. 1 (fall 1992): 47–49.

————. "Who Should Own the Schools?" *Equity and Choice* 9, no. 1 (fall 1992): 59–63.

_____. "What's Really at Stake in the School Choice Debate?" *Clearing House* 66, no. 2 (November–December 1992): 75–78.

_____. Review of *An Aristocracy of Everyone: The Politics of Education and the Future of America*, by Benjamin R. Barber. *First Things*, no. 32 (April 1993): 51–52.

_____. Review of *Why Johnny Can't Tell Right from Wrong*, by William Kilpatrick, and of *Reclaiming Our Schools: A Handbook on Teaching Character, Academics, and Discipline*, by Edward A. Wynne and Kevin Ryan. *First Things*, no. 35 (August–September 1993): 45–48.

_____. Review of *Battleground: The Religious Right, Its Opponents, and the Struggle for Our Schools*, by Stephen Bates. *First Things*, no. 39 (January 1994): 39–42.

_____. Review of *Public Education: An Autopsy*, by Myron Leiberman, and *The School-Choice Controversy: What Is Constitutional?* by James W. Skillen. *First Things*, no. 40 (February 1994): 46.

_____. "Massachusetts Models: Done Properly School Choice Can Promote Freedom and Equality." *Richmond Times Dispatch*, 18 May 1994: A13.

_____. "School Distinctiveness." *Journal of Education* 176, no. 2 (1994): 73–103.

_____. Review of *Battleground: One Mother's Crusade, the Religious Right, and the Struggle for Control of Our Classrooms*, by Stephen L. Bates. *Christian Scholar's Review* 24, no. 3 (1995): 344–46.

_____. *Educational Freedom in Eastern Europe.* Washington, DC: CATO Institute, 1995.

_____. "Choice and Distinctive Schools." *New Schools, New Communities* 12, no. 3 (spring 1996): 73–103.

_____. "Free Schools and the Revival of Urban Communities." In *Welfare in America: Christian Perspectives on a Policy in Crisis.* Ed. Stanley W. Carlson-Thies and James W. Skillen. Grand Rapids: Eerdmans Publishing, 1996.

_____. "What Would Equal Treatment Mean for Public Education?" In *Equal Treatment of Religion in a Pluralistic Society.* Ed. Stephen V. Monsma and J. Christopher Soper. Grand Rapids: Eerdmans Publishing, 1998.

_____. "Public School Choice: Searching for Direction." *Principal* 77, no. 5 (May 1998), 10–12.

_____. "What Real Education Requires." *Journal of Education* 180, no. 3 (1998), 41–50.

_____. *The Ambiguous Embrace: Government and Faith-Based Schools and Social Agencies.* Princeton, NJ: Princeton University Press, 2000.

Glenn, Charles Leslie, and Christine H. Rossel. "The Cambridge Controlled Choice Plan." *Urban Review* 20, no. 2 (summer 1988): 75–94.

Glenn, Charles Leslie, and Joshua L. Glenn. "Making Room for Religious Conviction in Democracy's Schools." In *Schooling Christians: "Holy Experiments" in American Education.* Ed. Stanley Hauerwas and John H. Westerhoff. Grand Rapids: Eerdmans Publishing, 1992.

Goodlad, John I., ed. *The Moral Dimensions of Teaching.* San Francisco: Jossey-Bass Publishers, 1990.

Graham, W. Fred. *The Constructive Revolutionary: John Calvin and His Socio-Economic Impact.* Atlanta: John Knox Press, 1978.

Gustafson, James M. *Protestant and Roman Catholic Ethics: Prospects for Rapprochement.* Chicago: University of Chicago Press, 1978.

———. *Ethics from a Theocentric Perspective.* Vol. 1, *Theology and Ethics.* Chicago: University of Chicago Press, 1981.

———. "The Sectarian Temptation: Reflections on Theology, The Church and the University." In *The Catholic Theological Society of America's Proceedings of the Fortieth Annual Convention.* Ed. George Kilcourse. Vol. 40 (5–8 June, 1985).

Harmin, Merrill, Howard Kirschenbaum, and Sidney B. Simon. *Clarifying Values Through Subject Matter: Applications for the Classroom.* Minneapolis: Winston Press, 1973.

Hauerwas, Stanley, and John H. Westerhoff, eds. *Schooling Christians: "Holy Experiments" in American Education.* Grand Rapids: Eerdmans Publishing, 1992.

Henig, Jeffery R. *Rethinking School Choice: Limits of the Market Metaphor.* Princeton, NJ: Princeton University Press, 1994.

Heslep, Robert D. *Moral Education for America.* Westport, CT: Praeger Publishers, 1995.

Hirsch, E. D. *Cultural Literacy: What Every American Needs to Know.* Boston: Hougton Mifflin, 1987.

Hewlett, Sylvia Ann. *When the Bough Breaks: The Cost of Neglecting Our Children.* New York: Basic Books, 1991.

Howe, Leland W. "Team-It: An Instructional Strategy." *Clearing House* 45, no. 7 (March 1971): 444–46.

———. "Educating to Make a Difference." *Phi Delta Kappan* 52, no. 9 (May 1971): 547–49.

Howe, Leland W., Sidney B. Simon, and Howard Kirschenbaum. "Value Clarification: Strategies." *Journal of the National Center for Law-Focused Education* 2, no. 2 (May 1973): 38–39.

Howe, Leland W., and Larry J. Krafft. "Affective Education Guidelines." *NASSAP Bulletin* 58, no. 380 (March 1974): 37–43.

Howe, Leland W,. and Mary Martha Howe. *Personalizing Education: Values Clarification and Beyond.* New York: Hart Publishing, 1975.

Howe, Leland W,. and Gordon Hart. "Counseling with a Focus on Values." *Education* 97, no. 10 (spring 1977): 237–41.

Howe, Leland W., and Bernard Solomon. *How to Raise Children in a TV World.* New York: Hart Publishing, 1979.

Kaus, Mickey. *The End of Equality.* New York: Basic Books, 1992.

Kilpatrick, William. *Why Johnny Can't Tell Right from Wrong: And What We Can Do About It.* New York: Simon and Schuster, 1992.

Kirschenbaum, Howard, and Sidney B. Simon, eds. *Readings in Values Clarification.* Minneapolis: Winston Press, 1973.

Kirschenbaum, Howard. "In Defense of Values Clarification." Saratoga Springs, NY: National Humanistic Education Center, 1975.

Kirschenbaum, Howard, Merrill Harmin, Leland W. Howe, and Sidney B. Simon, eds. "In Defense of Values Clarification." *Phi Delta Kappan* 58, no. 10 (June 1977): 743–46.

Kozol, Jonathan. *Savage Inequalities: Children in America's Schools.* New York: Crown Publishers, 1991.

Krafft, Larry J., and Leland W. Howe. "Guidelines for Sensitivity Training in Your School." *Phi Delta Kappan* 53, no. 3 (November 1971): 179–80.

Lickona, Thomas. "Critical Issues in the Study of Moral Development and Behavior." In *Moral Development and Behavior: Theory, Research, and Social Issues.* New York: Holt, Rinehart and Winston, 1976.

―――――. "Research on Piaget's Theory of Moral Development." In *Moral Development and Behavior: Theory, Research, and Social Issues.* New York: Holt, Rinehart and Winston, 1976.

―――――. "Project Change: A Person-centered Approach to CBTE." *Journal of Teacher Education* 22, no. 2 (summer 1976): 122–28.

―――――. "How to Encourage Moral Development." *Learning* 5, no. 7 (March 1977): 36–43.

―――――. "Preparing Teachers to Be Moral Educators: A Neglected Duty." *New Directions for Higher Education,* no. 31 (1980): 51–64.

―――――. "Democracy, Cooperation, and Moral Education." In *Toward Moral and Religious Maturity: The First International Conference on Moral and Religious Development.* Ed. Charles Brussselmans. Morristown, NJ: Silver Burdett Company, 1980.

―――――. "What Does Moral Psychology Have to Say to the Teacher of Ethics?" In *Ethics Teaching in Higher Education.* Ed. Daniel Callahan and Sissela Bok, 4:101–32. New York: Plenum Press, 1980.

―――――. "Four Strategies for Fostering Character Development and Academics in Children." *Phi Delta Kappan* 69, no. 6 (February 1988): 419–23.

―――――. "Kohlberg and Moral Education: Back to Virtue." *Counseling and Values* 32, no. 3 (April 1988): 187–92.

―――――. "How Parents and Schools Can Work Together to Raise Moral Children." *Educational Leadership* 45, no. 8 (May 1988): 36–38.

―――――. "Educating the Moral Child." *Principal* 68, no. 3 (November 1988): 6–10.

_____. "Character Development in Elementary-Grade Children." *Religion and Public Education* 16, no. 3 (fall 1989): 409–17.

_____. *Educating for Character: How Schools Can Teach Respect and Responsibility.* New York: Bantam Books, 1991.

_____. "Creating a Moral Community in the Classroom." *Instructor* 103 (September 1993): 69–72.

_____. "The Return of Character Education." *Educational Leadership* 51, no. 3 (November 1993): 6–11.

_____. "Where Sex Education Went Wrong." *Educational Leadership* 51, no. 3 (November. 1993): 84–89.

_____. "Is Character Education a Responsibility of the Public Schools? Yes." *Momentum* 24, no. 4 (November–December 1993): 48–54.

_____. "The Neglected Heart: The Emotional Dangers of Premature Sexual Involvement." *American Educator* 18, no. 2 (summer 1994): 34–39.

_____. *Raising Good Children: Helping Your Child Through the Stages of Moral Development.* New York: Bantam Books, 1994.

_____. *Sex, Love, and You: Making the Right Decision.* Notre Dame, IN: Ave Maria Press, 1994.

_____. "The Teacher's Role in Character Education." *Journal of Education* 179, no. 2 (1997), 63–79.

_____. "A More Complex Analysis Is Needed." *Phi Delta Kappan* 79, no. 1 (February 1998): 449–54.

_____. "Character Education: Seven Crucial Issues." *Action-in-Teacher-Education* 20, no. 4 (winter 1998), 77–84.

_____. "Religion and Character Education." *Phi Delta Kappan* 80, no. 1 (September 1999): 21–27.

_____. "Character Education: The Heart of School Reform." *Religion and Education* 27, no. 1 (fall 2000): 58–64.

Lieberman, Myron. *Public Education: An Autopsy.* Cambridge: Harvard University Press, 1993.

Lugo, Luis E., ed. *Religion, Pluralism, and Public Life: Abraham Kuyper's Legacy for the Twenty-First Century.* Grand Rapids: Eerdmans Publishing, 2000.

McCarthy, Rockne, James W. Skillen, and William Harper, eds. *Disestablishment a Second Time: Genuine Pluralism for America Schools.* Ann Arbor: University Microfilms International, 1995.

May, William F. *The Physician's Covenant: Images of the Healer in Medical Ethics.* Philadelphia: Westminster Press, 1983.

Merton, Robert K. *The Sociology of Science: Theoretical and Empirical Investigations.* Ed. Norman W. Storer. Chicago: University of Chicago Press, 1973.

Michaelson, Robert. *Piety in the Public Schools: Trends and Issues in the Relationship between Religion and the Public School in the United States.* London: Macmillan, 1970.

Miller, Ronald, ed. *The Renewal of Meaning in Education: Responses to the Cultural and Ecological Crisis of Our Times.* Brandon, VT: Holistic Education Press, 1993.

Morken, Hubert, and Jo Rene Formicola. *The Politics of School Choice.* Oxford: Rowman & Littlefield Publishers, 1999.

Mouw, Richard J. "Some Reflections on Sphere Sovereignty." In *Religion, Pluralism, and Public Life: Abraham Kuyper's Legacy for the Twenty-First Century.* Ed. Luis E. Lugo. Grand Rapids: Eerdmans Publishing, 2000.

Niebuhr, Reinhold, "Religion and Education." *Religious Education.* 48, no. 5 (November–December, 1953): 371.

Neuhaus, Richard John, ed. *Democracy and the Renewal of Public Education.* Grand Rapids: Eerdmans Publishing, 1987.

Nord, Warren. *Religion and American Education: Rethinking a National Dilemma.* Chapel Hill: University of North Carolina Press, 1995.

Ottati, Douglas F. "Assessing Moral Arguments: A Study Paper," Union Theological Seminary, Richmond, VA. September 1987.

————. *Reforming Protestantism: Christian Commitment in Today's World.* Louisville: Westminster/John Knox Press, 1995.

Paris, David C. *Ideology and Educational Reform: Themes and Theories in Public Education.* San Francisco: Westview Press, 1995.

Porpora, Douglas V. *Landscapes of the Soul: The Loss of Moral Meaning in American Life.* New York: Oxford University Press, 2001.

Porterfield, Amanda. *The Transformation of American Religion: The Story of a Late Twentieth-Century Awakening.* New York: Oxford University Press, 2001.

Postman, Neil. *Amusing Ourselves to Death: Public Discourse in the Age of Show Business.* New York: Penguin Books, 1985.

————. *The End of Education: Redefining the Value of School.* New York: Alfred A. Knopf, 1995.

Potter, Ralph B. *War and Moral Discourse: An Introduction to Ethics.* Richmond, VA: John Knox Press, 1969.

Power, F. Clark, and Daniel K. Lapsley, eds. *The Challenge of Pluralism: Education, Politics, and Values.* Notre Dame: University of Notre Dame Press, 1992.

Purpel, David E. "Introduction." In *Schools and Meaning: Essays on the Moral Nature of Schooling.* Ed. David E. Purpel and H. Svi Shapiro. New York: University Press of America, 1985.

————. Review of *Schooling as a Ritual Performance,* by Peter McLaren. *Educational Theory* 38 (winter 1988): 155–63.

————. *The Moral and Spiritual Crisis in Education: A Curriculum for Justice and Compassion in Education.* New York: Bergin and Garvey Press, 1989.

————. "Education as Sacrament." *Independent School* 50 (spring 1991): 45–60.

_____. "Moral Education: An Idea Whose Time Has Gone." *Clearing House* 64 (May/June 1991): 309–12.

_____. Review of *Education and the Good Life: Beyond the National Curriculum*, by John Ponsford White. *Educational Studies* 23 (summer 1992): 195–200.

_____. "Educational Discourse and Global Crisis: What's a Teacher to Do?" In *Critical Social Issues in American Education: Toward the 21st Century*. Ed. David E. Purpel and Svi Shapiro. New York: Longman Publishing Group, 1993.

_____. "Holistic Education in a Prophetic Voice." In *The Renewal of Meaning in Education: Responses to the Cultural and Ecological Crisis of Our Times*. Ed. Ron Miller. Brandon, VT: Holistic Education Press, 1993.

_____. Review of *Critical Pedagogy: An Introduction*, by Barry Kanpol. *Educational Studies* 26 (fall 1995): 218–23.

_____. *Moral Outrage in Education*. New York: Peter Lang Publishing, 1999.

Purpel, David E., and Maurice Belanger. "Toward a Humanistic Curriculum Theory." In *Curriculum and the Cultural Revolution: A Book of Essays and Readings*. Ed. by David E. Purpel and Maurice Belanger. Berkeley: McCutchan Publishing, 1972.

Purpel, David E, and Maurice Belanger. "Conclusions and Implications." In *Curriculum and the Cultural Revolution: A Book of Essays and Readings*. Ed. David E. Purpel and Maurice Belanger. Berkeley: McCutchan Publishing, 1972.

Purpel, David E., and Kevin Ryan. "Moral Education: Where Sages Fear to Tread." *Phi Delta Kappan* 56, no. 10 (June 1975): 659–62.

Purpel, David E., and Kevin Ryan. "Moral Education: What Is It and Where Are We?" In *Moral Education ... It Comes with the Territory*. Ed. David E. Purpel and Kevin Ryan. Berkeley: McCutchan Publishing, 1976.

Purpel, David E., and Kevin Ryan. "It Comes with the Territory: The Inevitability of Moral Education in the Schools." In *Moral Education ... It Comes with the Territory*.

Purpel, David E., and Kevin Ryan. "Moral Education in the Classroom: Some Instructional Issues." In *Moral Education . . . It Comes with the Territory*.

Purpel, David E., and Kevin Ryan. "What Can Be Done?" In *Moral Education ... It Comes with the Territory*.

Purpel, David E., and Henry Giroux. "Preface." In *The Hidden Curriculum and Moral Education: Deception or Discovery?* Ed. David E. Purpel and Henry Giroux. Berkeley: McCutchan Publishing, 1983.

Purpel, David E., and James B. MacDonald. "Curriculum and Planning: Visions and Metaphors." *Journal of Curriculum and Supervision* 2, no. 2 (winter 1987): 178–92.

Purpel, David E., and Svi Shapiro. *Beyond Liberation and Excellence: Reconstructing the Public Discourse on Education*. Westport, CT: Bergin and Garvey Press, 1995.

Putman, Robert D. *Bowling Alone: The Collapse and Revival of American Community*. New York: Simon & Schuster, 2000.

Rathbone, Christina. *On the Outside Looking In: A Year in an Inner-City High School*. New York: Atlantic Monthly Press, 1998.

Ravitch, Diane. *The Troubled Crusade: American Education 1945–1980*. New York: Basic Books, 1983.

_____. *The Schools We Deserve: Reflections on the Educational Crises of Our Time*. New York: Basic Books, 1985.

Rawls, John. *Political Liberalism*. New York: Columbia University Press, 1993.

Roberts, Raymond R. "Renewing Public School Teaching as a Christian Vocation." *The Presbyterian Outlook*. 170, no. 15 (5 May 1977): 8–9.

Robertson, Pat. *Answers to 200 of Life's Most Probing Questions*. Nashville: Thomas Nelson Publishers, 1984.

_____. *The New Millennium: 10 Trends that Will Impact You and Your Family by the Year 2000*. Dallas: Word Publishing, 1990.

_____. *The New World Order*. Dallas: Word Publishing, 1991.

_____. *The Secret Kingdom: Your Path to Love, Peace, and Financial Security*. Dallas: Word Publishing, 1992.

_____. *The Turning Tide*. Dallas: Word Publishing, 1993.

Roof, Wade Clark. *Spiritual Marketplace: Baby Boomers and the Remaking of American Religion*. Princeton, NJ: Princeton University Press, 1999.

Ryan, Kevin. "The Search for Values." *The Merrow Report* (fall–winter 1993–94).

Ryan, Kevin, and Edward A. Wynne. *Reclaiming Our Schools: A Handbook on Teaching Character, Academics, and Discipline*. New York: Merrill, 1993.

Sandel, Michael J. *Democracy's Discontent: America in Search of a Public Philosophy*. Cambridge: Belknap Press of Harvard University Press, 1996.

Sandin, Robert T. *The Rehabilitation of Virtue: Foundations of Moral Education*. New York: Praeger Publishers, 1992.

Shanker, Albert. "Down the Tubes?" *The New Republic*, (6 November 1995): 23.

Simon, Sidney B., Leland W. Howe, and Howard Kirschenbaum. *Values Clarification*. New York: Warner Books, 1995.

Skillen, James W. *Recharging the American Experiment: Principled Pluralism for Genuine Civic Community*. Grand Rapids: Baker Books, 1994.

Spring, Joel. *Political Agendas for Education: From the Christian Coalition to the Green Party*. Mahwah, NJ: Lawrence Erlbaum Associates, 1997.

Stackhouse, Max L. *Creeds, Society and Human Rights: A Study in Three Cultures*. Grand Rapids: Eerdmans Publishing, 1984.

_____. "An Ecumenist's Plea for a Public Theology." *This World* no. 8 (spring/summer 1984).

_____. *Public Theology and Political Economy: Christian Stewardship in Modern Society.* New York: University Press of America, 1991.

Stackhouse, Max L., and Peter J. Paris, eds. Vol. 1, *God and Globalization: Theological Ethics and the Spheres of Life.* Harrisburg, PA: Trinity Press International, 2000.

Stackhouse, Max L., and Don S. Browning, eds. Vol. 2, *God and Globalization: The Spirit and the Modern Authorities.* Harrisburg, PA: Trinity Press International, 2001.

Stein, Rita, Roberta Richin, Richard Banyon, Francine Banyon, and Marc Stein. *Connecting Character to Conduct: Helping Students Do the Right Things.* Alexandria, VA: Association for Supervision and Curriculum Development, 2000.

Stevenson, Harold W., and James W. Stigler. *The Learning Gap: Why Our Schools Are Failing and What We Can Learn from Japanese and Chinese Education.* New York: Summit Books, 1992.

Sullivan, Andrew. "TRB from Washington: Watch It." *The New Republic* (30 April 2001): 8.

Sunseri, Ron. *Outcome-Based Education: Understanding the Truth about Education Reform.* Sisters, OR: Multnomah Books, 1994.

Swezey, Charles Mason. "What is Theological Ethics? A Study of the Thought of James M. Gustafson." Ph.D. diss., Vanderbilt University, 1978.

Tillich, Paul. *Systematic Theology.* Vol. 1, *Reason and Revelation.* Chicago: University of Chicago Press, 1951.

Toch, Thomas. *In the Name of Excellence: The Struggle to Reform the Nation's Schools, Why It's Failing, and What Should Be Done.* New York: Oxford, 1991.

Trend, David. *The Crisis of Meaning in Culture and Education.* Minneapolis: University of Minnesota Press, 1995.

Troeltsch, Ernst. *The Social Teaching of the Christian Churches,* Vol. 1. Louisville: Westminster/John Knox Press, 1992.

Vincent, Dr. Philip Fitch. *Promising Practices in Character Education: Nine Success Stories from Around the Country.* Chapel Hill, NC: Character Development Publishing, 1996.

_____. *Rules and Procedures for Character Education: The First Step toward School Civility.* Chapel Hill, NC: Character Development Publishing, 1999.

Volokh, Eugene, "Vouched For: School Choice is Constitutional." *The New Republic* (6 July 1998): 12–14.

Walsh, David. *The Growth of the Liberal Soul.* Columbia, MO: University of Missouri Press, 1997.

Walzer, Michael. *Spheres of Justice: A Defense of Pluralism and Equality.* New York: Basic Books, 1983.

———. *Thick and Thin: Moral Argument at Home and Abroad.* Notre Dame, IN: University of Notre Dame Press, 1994.

Ward, Leo R. "The Right to Religious Literacy." *Religious Education,* 48 (November–December, 1953): 380.

Wolfe, David E., and Leland W. Howe. "Personalizing Foreign Language Instruction." *Journal: Foreign Language Instruction Annals* 7, no. 1 (October 1973): 81–90.

INDEX

abortion, 24
abstinence, 41
academic freedom, 114, 118
Adams, James Luther, 108
Africa, 88
Afrocentric critics, 13, 14n
Allen, Jeanne, 2
Ambiguous Embrace, The, by Glenn, 21
anthropological assumptions:
  philosophy of religion
  first element of moral reasoning, 5
  religion features prominently in the five writers', 61
  underlying the theory of spheres, 121
aptitude, 123
Aristotle, 119
atheism, atheists, 34, 42, 43
"at risk" children, 130
Ayre, A. J., 11

Baals, the ancient, 35
Babel, Tower of, 113
ballet lessons, 115
Barbour, Ian, 42
Bennett, William, 2
Bible, 10, 34, 36, 50, 53, 74, 128
Black, Hugo, 105
Bonhoeffer, Dietrich, 108, 119
Buchanan, Pat, 6
Bush, George W., 1, 14, 64, 88, 119

Calvin, John, 128
Calvinists, 53
categorical imperative, 38

Catholicism, 10, 14, 40, 42, 53, 70, 98, 99
Center for Education Reform, 2
character 13, 14, 19, 20, 23, 24, 26, 29, 33, 35, 37, 38, 39, 40, 43, 56, 69, 72, 73, 75, 76, 77, 78, 82, 89, 98, 116
character education movement, 13–14, 24, 26
charismatic leadership: one of six authorities (derivative spheres), 109
charter schools, 1, 2, 14, 62, 123
chastity, 41, 99
Christ, 120, 121
"Christian nation," 12
Christian religious right, 12, 13, 14, 15, 17, 18, 60, 61
Christian values, 4, 12, 15, 17, 18, 22, 51, 62, 85, 86
church, 10, 49, 55, 56, 83, 87, 90, 110, 113, 115, 119, 127, 128
church-run schools. *See* faith-based schools
civic virtue, 21, 54
civil religion, 42, 43, 46, 104, 118
civil rights, 11, 65, 95
Civil War, 95
class discrimination, 14
Clinton, Bill, 88
Colossians, 120
Columbine High School, 3, 13
commercial child and youth culture, 125
common faith, 10, 83
common good, 67, 101, 123, 125, 129